T0358279

Disaster Resilience and Sustainability

This book examines urban planning and infrastructure development in Japanese cities after the Second World War as a way to mitigate the risks of disasters while pursuing sustainable development. It looks at the benefits of social capital and how communities organise to tackle problems during the recovery phase after a disaster. The book also illustrates these issues with case studies to highlight community attitudes which improve recovery outcomes.

The book underlines challenges such as ageing and depopulation, which Japan would face should the next disaster occur. These demographic shifts are causing difficulties among neighbourhood associations at a time when communities need to effectively support each other. Nakanishi explains why overcoming these societal issues is imperative for sustainability and the need for a comprehensive approach which would integrate smart technology.

This book will be of interest to scholars in city development and planning, urban studies and human geography as well as those interested in building resilient communities.

Hitomi Nakanishi is Associate Professor of Built Environment at the University of Canberra, Australia.

Routledge Research in Sustainable Planning and Development in Asia
Series Editor: Richard Hu

Urban Flood Risk Management
Looking at Jakarta
Christopher Silver

Data-centric Regenerative Built Environment
Big Data for Sustainable Regeneration
Saeed Banihashemi and Sepideh Zarepour Sohi

Disaster Resilience and Sustainability
Japan's Urban Development and Social Capital
Hitomi Nakanishi

For more information about this series, please visit: www.routledge.com/
Routledge-Research-in-Sustainable-Planning-and-Development-in-Asia/
book-series/RRSPDA

Disaster Resilience and Sustainability

Japan's Urban Development and Social Capital

Hitomi Nakanishi

Routledge
Taylor & Francis Group

LONDON AND NEW YORK

First published 2023
by Routledge
4 Park Square, Milton Park, Abingdon, Oxon OX14 4RN

and by Routledge
605 Third Avenue, New York, NY 10158

Routledge is an imprint of the Taylor & Francis Group, an informa business

British Library Cataloguing-in-Publication Data
A catalogue record for this book is available from the British Library

Library of Congress Cataloging-in-Publication Data
Names: Nakanishi, Hitomi, author.
Title: Disaster resilience and sustainability : Japan's urban development and social capital / Hitomi Nakanishi.
Description: Abingdon, Oxon ; New York, NY : Routledge, 2023. | Series: Routledge research in sustainable planning and development in Asia | Includes bibliographical references and index. |
Identifiers: LCCN 2022021075 (print) | LCCN 2022021076 (ebook) | ISBN 9780367712914 (hardback) | ISBN 9780367712921 (paperback) | ISBN 9781003150190 (ebook)
Subjects: LCSH: City planning—Japan—Case studies. | Hazard mitigation—Japan—Case studies. | Infrastructure (Economics)—Japan—Case studies. | Sustainable urban development—Japan—Case studies. | Natural disasters—Japan—Case studies.
Classification: LCC HT169.J3 N3539 2023 (print) | LCC HT169.J3 (ebook) | DDC 307.1/2160952—dc23/eng/20220610
LC record available at https://lccn.loc.gov/2022021075
LC ebook record available at https://lccn.loc.gov/2022021076

ISBN: 9780367712914 (hbk)
ISBN: 9780367712921 (pbk)
ISBN: 9781003150190 (ebk)

DOI: 10.4324/9781003150190

Typeset in Times New Roman
by Apex CoVantage, LLC

Contents

Figures

Tables

Acknowledgements

Many people contributed to the production of this book. This book would never have been possible without encouragement and advice from many survivors in North East Japan (*Tohoku*) whom I met through my fieldwork during the last ten years. There are many people to thank in *Tohoku*, but seven people must be acknowledged at the outset. Yoshihisa Nishikawa, Takenori Osu, Mitsuko Osu, Shunichiro Fujimura, Koji Shidara, Naomasa Tanabe and Miori Kashima gave me generous support for my research. We published the book *Surviving the 2011 Tsunami:100 Testimonies of Ishinomaki Area Survivors of the Great East Japan Earthquake* (Junposha Publishing Co., Ltd.) in 2014 to disseminate survivors' stories to the world. Mihoko Terada, Ryoko Endo and Shinichi Endo were also great supporters. Ryoko Endo came to Sydney in 2018 when we organised a film exhibition of 'Life Goes On' featuring the recovery of *Tohoku*. Yukiko Hirano and Misaki Ito and their team for the Rainbow Project, Japan Club of Sydney, supported the film exhibition. Yoji Kagawa, a member of the city council of Takamatsu, connected me with community leaders and provided me with photos taken by residents. Associate Professors Naoto Tanaka, Yukiko Takeuchi and Yuji Hoshino, Kumamoto University, provided valuable comments on the recovery of Kumamoto after the 2016 earthquakes. Kimiharu Saita advised me on the meteorological system that causes typhoons and heavy rains.

I thank my research collaborators Professor Yoshihiro Suenaga, Kagawa University, Associate Professor Sarah Wise, University College London and Associate Professor Yasuko Hassall Kobayashi, Ritsumeikan University, who provided collaborative efforts and valuable advice. We continue working together in disaster research.

Grants and financial support came from diverse sources to support my research. The University of Canberra, Kagawa University, the Obayashi Foundation, the Toyota Foundation, the Murata Foundation and Urban

Research and Planning (URaP) International supported my research over the ten years.

I received great support from senior academics, who are my long-term supervisors and mentors. I thank Emeritus Professor John Andrew Black, University of New South Wales (UNSW), who was one of the supervisors of my PhD as well as a research collaborator since I became an academic. Professor Barbara Norman, University of Canberra, Professor Deborah Blackman, UNSW Canberra, Professor Michael Batty, University College London and Dr Mina Matsudaira are also acknowledged for their mentoring, advice and support. Professor Kenji Doi, Osaka University and Emeritus Professor Katsuhiko Kuroda, Kobe University also continued to support my research activities over the years. Members of the Urban Environmental Management Study Group in Kansai region are also acknowledged for inspiration.

For the production process of this book, I thank Kendrick Loo, the editor from Routledge, for advice on the publication process. I also thank two anonymous reviewers who provided valuable feedback to my proposal. Professor Richard Hu, University of Canberra, who is the series editor, is acknowledged. Pauline Busch and Satomi Trevaskis assisted me in searching for and collecting literature and proofreading.

None of my research would have been possible without the support of my husband, Jeffrey Busch. Finally, I dedicate this book to my parents, who greatly supported me to become an academic and encouraged my school and university education. My father drove me to many fieldwork sites and interview venues so that I could focus on my work as much as possible. They have been great supporters and at the same time, valuable advisors who have residents' perspectives.

1 Introduction

On 11 March 2011, around 16:30pm (Australian Eastern Daylight Time [AEDT]), I came home and was reading an off-print copy of my new journal article. I was temporarily living with my parents-in-law at that time. After around 30 minutes, my mother-in-law came from her study and told me 'I think you should rush to a TV and watch the news. The radio news I was listening to reported that there was a big earthquake in Japan.' I grew up in Japan, therefore, I was used to seeing the news about earthquakes, but this time sounded very different. The earthquake that had occurred two weeks before in Christchurch was still fresh in my memory. I rushed to a TV room and turned on ABC[1] news. The screen was showing footage of tsunami waves bigger than I had seen before. An anchor was explaining that waves were reaching the North East coast of Japan and the footage was taken from a helicopter of Japan's defence force. Both my parents-in-law joined me, and we just kept watching the waves, holding our breath. We could see many cars stranded and washed away. We just hoped that what we were watching was not true. After a while, many reports started being posted on the internet, but it looked like the whole picture of the disaster was yet to be understood. I had a friend in Ibaragi prefecture and sent a message to him, but there was still no response when I went to bed. The next morning, the Japanese newspapers were full of shocking articles and figures. The media started to focus on the Fukushima Daiichi nuclear power plant, which was in crisis. I finally received a reply from my friend saying he was safe but had no access to utilities. I was also informed that the communication network was severely affected by the earthquake and tsunami. I talked with my parents who lived in the southern part of Japan. They were not affected but were concerned about the victims and the nuclear power plant. The aftershocks were continuing.

As an academic in urban/transport planning and infrastructure development, my research had focused on people's travel behaviours and how infrastructure could make transport efficient, with more environmentally friendly

DOI: 10.4324/9781003150190-1

Figure 1.1 Devastation after the North East Japan earthquake and tsunami 2011
Source: (taken by the author in September, 2011)

options. I did not expect that I would be involved in disaster research when I was a PhD student. However, I had an opportunity to visit the affected area in September 2011 after attending an international conference in Tokyo. A professor at the Tohoku Institute of Technology kindly guided me to the Oritate and Natori areas in and around Sendai city. It was six months after the event and there were still mountains of debris and partially damaged houses were untouched.

The next day, I went to Ishinomaki. My friend from high school established a volunteer organisation to help affected communities. I was invited by her to do fieldwork in Ishinomaki. Because the Japan Railway (JR) was damaged between Sendai and Ishinomaki, we needed to use a car. Luckily, we were offered seats in a TV crew's vehicle. The roads from Ishinomaki to Sendai were damaged by the earthquake and liquefaction. There were many trucks going north bringing materials for reconstruction work. Therefore, the trip took us longer than we thought (around three hours; it usually takes about an hour to drive from Sendai to Ishinomaki). In Ishinomaki, I saw more devastation. I could visit temporary housing sites and had opportunities to listen to the narratives of survivors. A survivor invited me to dinner, saying, 'Since my husband was washed away, I have had no one to cook for, so it is a pleasure to have someone.' The homemade cuisine using local vegetables and fish was absolutely delicious, but I felt sad imagining there would be thousands of people like this lady. Each story was shocking and devastating, and I could not listen without tears, but it was important for me to understand the situation, as I had never experienced a tsunami myself. This visit was a turning point for me as a scholar in urban planning. Since then, I became more interested in urban disaster management and disaster risk reduction. After my first visit, I was invited to participate in a local research team investigating a community bus service for residents living in temporary housing. This was my first research conducted in the area of disaster risk reduction and resilience. My second visit to the affected area was in January of 2012. Since then, I have visited the site every year, and until 2019, I had visited the site ten times to do fieldwork, administer questionnaire surveys and conduct interviews with affected residents and the authorities in charge of recovery. I also did some work in Christchurch, New Zealand and in other parts of Japan, extending my knowledge of natural hazards and disaster risk reduction. When I was conducting fieldwork intensively in the tsunami-devastated area of North East Japan, I was often encouraged by survivors' words: 'Please share our lessons to the world and help them to prepare, so that they can minimise the number of people who die or suffer from natural hazards.'

Japan is one of the most hazard prone countries in the world. Natural hazards occur successively – another disaster often happens even before the recovery from the previous one is complete. Our urban environment is always in the process of recovering from disasters and adapting to new circumstances by enhancing resilience. A definition of disaster resilience in the built environment is the 'ability/skills/knowledge to collectively act to use the physical and economic resources effectively and collectively to survive and function' (Nakanishi et al., 2014, p. 343). The aim of this book is to review and discuss how Japan, a natural hazard nation, has been adapting to cascading hazards since the reconstruction after the Second World War. I also discuss current societal issues and future challenges that have significant implications for urban development.

This book is structured as follows. In the following chapter, I explain post-war urban planning and infrastructure development. Japanese cities sustained catastrophic damage due to bombing and the absence of upkeep during the war. Five comprehensive national development plans were developed in the following four decades to support post-war recovery, economic growth and the balanced distribution of industry and infrastructure across the country. As a disaster-prone country, buildings and infrastructure have been designed and maintained to be resistant to earthquakes, floods, tsunamis and typhoons. Major natural hazards after World War II are also reviewed and their impact on disaster risk reduction is discussed. Chapter 3 focuses on the society of Japan, which has been responding to and recovering from the impact of natural hazards over time. Disaster resilience is not just about building hard infrastructure and urban systems. It is also about the capacity of residents and communities to cope with unexpected incidents, chaos and the prolonged process of recovery. Chapter 3 highlights how Japanese communities have fostered social capital as a vital infrastructure to respond to natural hazards. The transition of society and current challenges are also discussed. Chapters 4–6 provide case studies of three major natural hazards: a typhoon, an earthquake and a flood. Chapter 4 focuses on the typhoons of 2004, which caused a record-breaking storm surge in the Seto Inland Sea. Japan has on average 20 typhoons passing every year, causing heavy rain, floods and landslides across the country. Not all typhoons significantly impact communities, and many people are unprepared in this area of Japan. However, this perception needs to change. By examining the responses of the driest city in Japan to the 2004 typhoons, the author asserts that raising awareness is still key to minimising the risks. In Chapter 5, the case of the 2016 Kumamoto earthquake is discussed. In this chapter, the author focuses on the collaborative actions of government, community and local universities in managing recovery and long-term challenges. Chapter 6 focuses on the increasing risk of heavy rain and floods. The 2018 Western Japan flood case is reviewed and ways to enhance preparedness are discussed. In Chapter 7, the concept of Society 5.0, a new plan for an 'information society,' and its relationship to disaster resilience is discussed. The impact of the COVID-19 pandemic (SARS-CoV-2) is examined and insights into a sustainable future are provided. In conclusion, the core value of urban development and management to enhance resilience is suggested. The information and photos used in this book were collected by the author[2] through fieldwork and interviews with residents, practitioners and scholars. Many scholarly references are cited, but academic theories and jargon presented in this book are kept to a minimum for a wider audience.

Notes

1 Australian Broadcasting Corporation.
2 Photo 4.1 was provided by a resident. All other photos were taken by the author.

Reference

Nakanishi, H., Black, J., & Matsuo, K. (2014). Disaster resilience in transportation: Japan earthquake and tsunami 2011. *International Journal of Disaster Resilience in the Built Environment, 5*(4), 341–361. https://doi.org/10.1108/IJDRBE-12-2012-0039

2 Japan's urban planning and infrastructure development after WWII

Recovery from post-war devastation and urban development

Japanese cities were devastated by incendiary bombs in the last two years of WWII (Sorensen, 2002). More than 10 million people were affected (including 1 million injured and 0.6 million dead). This was in addition to more than 3 million people who perished in the war and around 331,000 civilians who died (Honda et al., 1995; Sorensen, 2002). About 63,150 hectares were burned in the 115 cities. These cities were included in reconstruction planning.

After the war, there was a serious shortage of dwellings because many people lost their homes to fire. The reconstruction phase started during America's five years of occupation of Japan, led by General Douglas MacArthur. The War Damage Reconstruction Board (*Sensai Fukko In*) was established (Asano, 2012; Sorensen, 2002). During this period, a Basic Policy for War-damaged Areas Reconstruction (*Sensaichi Fukko Keikaku Kihon Houshin*) and the National Land Planning Basic Policy (*Kokudo Keikaku Kihon Houshin*) were developed in 1945, followed by guidelines for National Land Reconstruction (*Fukko Kokudo Keikaku Youkou*) and the Special City Planning Act (*Tokubetsu Toshi Keikaku Ho*) in 1946 (Kawakami, 1995; Sorensen, 2002). The most devastated cities were located on the national spine of Japan that connects the three metropolitan areas of Tokyo, Osaka and Nagoya (Honda et al., 1995). Each city approached the Ministry of Home Affairs to discuss reconstruction planning soon after the end of the war, leading to the aforementioned 'Basic Policy for War-damaged Areas Reconstruction' on 30 December 1945 (Asano, 2012). Other issues in the aftermath of the war were the shortage of food, flood management infrastructure and securing energy for industrialisation. This led to the development of hydro-electric generation and dams (Yada, 2014). The purpose of these reconstruction efforts was to bring rapid economic growth, which was the first priority for post-war recovery.

In 1950, the National Land Comprehensive Development Law (*Kokudo Sougou Kaihatsu Ho*) was implemented. The five themes for the development

DOI: 10.4324/9781003150190-2

under this law were 1) to utilise natural resources such as land and water, 2) to enhance preparedness for natural hazards, 3) a balanced allocation of urban areas and rural villages across the country, 4) a balanced allocation of industry across the country and 5) investment in infrastructure and the communication network in a way that did not impinge upon tourism destinations (Maeda et al., 1995). The industrial spine, which is also known as the 'Pacific Belt' along the Tokaido Corridor (Sorensen, 2002), was the priority area for urbanisation and population growth. The development of the Tokaido Corridor[1] (i.e., Pacific Belt) was supported by the development of the two main projects of transport infrastructure, that is, high-speed rail (*Shinkansen*) and the Tomei expressway (Nakanishi & Kurauchi, 2021). Development was completed by the end of the 1960s. Japan experienced such rapid economic growth that the national government declared 'it is no longer post-war' in the Economic White Paper (*Keizai Hakusho*) in 1956. The Tokyo Olympic Games in 1964 was a milestone event for Japan, allowing the country to showcase its recovery and rapid economic growth to the rest of the world. The population grew along with the economic growth and became concentrated in urban areas of the 'Pacific Belt.' As of 2020, the population on the 'Pacific Belt' area was over 66.5 million and its annual GDP was similar to the GDP of the United Kingdom (Black, 2022).

Table 2.1 Summary of the five comprehensive national development plans

Comprehensive National Development Plan (1962)	Development of industrial zones.
New Comprehensive National Development Plan (1969)	Investment in infrastructure such as high-speed rail, expressways, airports, bridges and tunnels that link the mainland and other islands. Investment in information and communication networks.
The Third Comprehensive National Development Plan (1977)	Enhancement of the living environment of citizens, improvement of the welfare system, regional development (including economic development of regional areas).
The Fourth Comprehensive National Development Plan (1987)	Development of mid- and small-sized cities, further development of transportation infrastructure and communication networks.
The Fifth Comprehensive National Development Plan 'Grand Design for the 21st Century' (1998)	National land conservation and management, improvement of quality of life, enhancement of transportation systems and communication infrastructure.

(Source: Author's compilation from Yamada (1994); Yada (2014); Ministry of Land, Infrastructure, Transport and Tourism (1998))

The five comprehensive national development plans (CNDPs; approved by the Japanese Cabinet in 1962, 1969, 1977, 1987 and 1998 respectively) were developed from the 1960s until the late 1990s to provide the key principles of national land use planning.

In the 1970s, when the Third Comprehensive National Development Plan was developed, the focus shifted to the management of land (including the improvement of the living environment and preparation for natural hazard) (Yada, 2014). This shift was triggered by the oil shock and a growing awareness of environmental pollution resulting from rapid growth. The government was also concerned about the divide between urban and rural areas as people flocked to the three metropolitan cities (Tokyo, Osaka and Nagoya), which became the centres of economic activities. The government, after the third plan, began to invest in regional areas. However, drift to the cities did not stop. The population of Tokyo accelerated even after 2010, whilst in rural areas, the young population decreased and the proportion of older people increased.

Natural hazards after World War II

Whilst Japan's economy was rapidly recovering and more investment in infrastructure was made, natural hazards continuously affected its society. Table 2.2 shows major hazards that occurred after the World War II.

Table 2.2 Major disasters after WWII

Year	Disaster	Summary of impact
1945	Makurazaki typhoon	On 17 September, this typhoon landed on Makurazaki, Kagoshima prefecture. The typhoon moved from south to north Japan, causing heavy rain and more than 2,000 people dead/missing.
1946	Nankaido earthquake	A magnitude 8 earthquake occurred on 21 December. Deaths: 1,342, houses destroyed: 14,259. Dykes, revetment and port related facilities were damaged on the Pacific Ocean side of Shikoku, Kii peninsula and Awaji Island.
1959	Isewan typhoon	On 26 September, the typhoon landed on the Shiono cape of Wakayama prefecture. This typhoon was characterised by its strong wind (recorded instantaneous wind speed was 55.3m/sec). The storm surge caused serious inundation in wider areas. Deaths: more than 4,600, missing: more than 400, number of flooded houses: more than 363,600.

(*Continued*)

Table 2.2 (Continued)

Year	Disaster	Summary of impact
1961	Second Muroto typhoon	On 16 September, the typhoon landed on the Muroto cape, Kochi prefecture. The recorded instantaneous wind speed was above 84.5m/sec. The storm surge inundated the west to central area of Osaka (over 31km^2). Deaths: 194, missing: 8, number of flooded houses: 384,120.
1976	The 17th typhoon[2]	On 13 September, the typhoon landed on Nagasaki prefecture and headed towards the north. It brought heavy rain recording 500–1,000mm (in west Japan) and 2,000mm (Shikoku), floods and landslides. Dykes of the Nagara River were broken in Gifu prefecture. Deaths: 161, missing: 10, number of flooded houses: 534,495.
1991	Typhoons 17, 18 and 19	Three typhoons landed in Japan successively during 12–15 September (17th typhoon), 17–20 September (18th typhoon) and 25–28 September (19th typhoon). The 19th typhoon had strong wind and caused storm surges. The impact on agricultural products was significant. Deaths: 84, missing: 2, number of flooded houses: 89,400.
1993	Heavy rain	Heavy rain was brought by a stagnant front during 31 July–1 August and 9–10 August (associated with the 7th typhoon). It also rained 26–27 August. Floods and landslides occurred in the southern part of Kyushu. Deaths and missing: 93, number of flooded houses: 16,496.
1995	Hanshin Awaji (Kobe) earthquake	On 17 January at 5:46, a magnitude 7.3 earthquake hit the southern area of Hyogo prefecture. It was the first earthquake in Japanese history that directly hit a metropolitan area (Kobe) and caused the maximum number of casualties. Deaths: 6,434, injured: 43,792, houses completely destroyed: 104,906, houses partly destroyed: 144,274, houses burnt: 7,132.
1999	The 18th typhoon	On 24 September, the typhoon landed in the north of Kumamoto prefecture and headed towards the Japan Sea. The typhoon brought heavy rain to wider areas. A storm surge occurred in the Seto Inland area of Kyushu and Shikoku, killing 12 people in Kumamoto. A tornado that occurred in Toyohashi caused many injuries. Deaths: 31, injured: 1,218, number of flooded houses: 19,650.

Year	Disaster	Summary of impact
2004	Heavy rain	A seasonal rain front stretched over the Japan Sea to northeast Japan, bringing heavy rain on 12–13 July. The record-breaking rain was observed in Tochio, Niigata (421mm) and Tadami and in Fukushima (325mm). Deaths: 16, number of flooded houses: 8,177.
2004	The 16th typhoon	The typhoon landed on Kagoshima on 30 August and crossed Kyushu, then moved towards the northeast and Hokkaido. It brought heavy rain to the Pacific Ocean side (more than 500mm). It was on the spring tide and the highest tide level was recorded in the Seto Inland Sea area. Deaths: 14, number of flooded houses: 46,220.
2004	The 23rd typhoon	The typhoon crossed across West Japan during 19–21 October. It brought heavy rain which caused landslides in various places, leading to high casualties. Deaths: 95, number of flooded houses: 54,743.
2004	Niigata Chuetsu earthquake	On 23 October at 17:56, a magnitude 6.8 earthquake hit the Chuetsu area of Niigata prefecture. *Shindo* 7 was recorded, which was the highest since the '*Shindo* measures'[3] were updated in 1996. Deaths: 68, injured: 4,814, houses completely destroyed: 3,174, houses partly destroyed: 119,492.
2005	Heavy snow	Record breaking snowfall was observed along the Japan Sea coast during December 2005 until March 2006. The average temperature in December was lowest since WWII. The record-breaking height of 416cm of snow was observed in Niigata on 5 February. Many people lost lives or were injured when they were removing snow. Deaths: 152, injured: 2,145.
2011	North East Japan earthquake and tsunami of 2011	On 11 March at 14:46, a magnitude 9 earthquake hit the North East coastal area of Japan (Tohoku region). The *Shindo* recorded was 7. The tsunami which followed the earthquake had an unprecedented impact on the affected area. The tsunami crippled the Fukushima nuclear power plant, which caused the leak of radioactive substances to the surrounding area.[4] The Prime Minister declared it 'the toughest and most difficult crisis for Japan in the 65 years after World War II.' At its peak level, 468,653 people were evacuated to shelters. Deaths:19,747, missing: 2,556, houses completely destroyed: 122,005, houses partly destroyed: 503,677.

(Continued)

Table 2.2 (Continued)

Year	Disaster	Summary of impact
2011	The 12th typhoon	The typhoon landed on Kochi and Okayama prefectures on 3 September and headed to the Japan Sea. The rainfall exceeded 1,000mm on the Kii peninsula during 30 August to 5 September. Floods and landslides occurred in various places in West Japan. Deaths: 82, number of flooded houses: 22,094.
2016	Kumamoto earthquake	On 14 April 2016 at 21:26, a magnitude 6.5 earthquake struck the Kumamoto region. Two days later on 16 April at 1:25, another shock (magnitude 7.3) struck the same area. Later, the second shock was determined as a 'main' shock by the Bureau of Meteorology. Also, 190 landslides were recorded. Deaths: 273, injured: 2,809, houses completely or partly destroyed: 163,500.
2017	North Kyushu heavy rain	A seasonal rain front and the 3rd typhoon brought heavy rain to West Japan. Deaths: 39, missing: 4, injured: 35, number of flooded houses: 1,908.
2018	The Western Japan floods	A seasonal rain front stayed over West Japan. Also, the 7th typhoon brought wet air to Japan, causing record-breaking heavy rain in the western part. The recorded rain volume from 28 June to 8 July was 1,800mm in Shikoku and 1,200 in the Tokai area. The floods and landslides caused a significant number of casualties and damage to infrastructure. Deaths: 224, missing: 8, injured: 459, number of flooded houses: 30,480.
2018	The 21st typhoon	On 4 September, the 21st typhoon landed on the south side of Tokushima, then landed again on Kobe by bringing strong wind, heavy rain and a storm surge. The recorded tidal height observed in Osaka was 329cm. The Kansai International Airport was flooded with major impacts on passenger flights, ferries and railway services due to the blackout of electricity and communication network.
2019	The 19th typhoon (East Japan typhoon)	On 6 October, the typhoon landed on the Izu peninsula, southwest of Tokyo, bringing heavy rain, strong wind, high tides and storm surges to the national capital region. The recorded tide height was 230cm (Tokyo) and record-breaking tidal height was observed in the surrounding region. Infrastructure was severely damaged including bullet train facilities. Deaths: 105, missing: 3, injured: 375.

Year	Disaster	Summary of impact
2020	Heavy rain	A seasonal rain front brought heavy rain all over Japan during 3–8 July. The most notable impact was the flooding of big rivers (Kuma River, Chikugo River etc.). The Kyushu area was most affected by floods and landslides. Deaths: 84, missing: 2, injured: 77, number of flooded houses: 6,971.

(Source: Made by author referring to Shikoku Disaster Information Archives: www.shikoku-saigai.com/ (in Japanese), the Disaster Archives (1945–2021) of Japan Meteorological Agency website (www.jma.go.jp/jma/indexe.html) (in Japanese) and the Fire and Disaster Management Agency website www.fdma.go.jp/ (in Japanese))

These are just major hazards and there were more of a smaller scale. In Japan, typhoons and earthquakes are common hazards, and smaller scale ones do not usually cause casualties, although infrastructure may sustain minor damages. Some major disasters have influenced the standard of infrastructure and the perceptions of citizens in managing natural hazards. For example, the Isewan typhoon was a turning point for the building code defined by The Architectural Insitute of Japan. They advised against wooden buildings, as they were more prone to fire, wind and flood damage caused by extreme natural hazards where risks are high (Architectural Institute of Japan, 2010).

After the Hanshin Awaji (Kobe) earthquake, the Japan Society of Civil Engineers proposed a) that earthquakes and earth-quake motions need to be considered in earthquake-resistant design, b) earthquake-resistant methods, c) aseismic diagnosis and aseismic reinforcement and d) general seismic safety planning. These modifications were suggested because the disaster had occurred in a densely populated urban centre where insufficient earthquake resistance had been incorporated into structures (Japan Society of Civil Engineers, n.d.).

It was after the North East Japan earthquake and tsunami of 2011 that disaster risk reduction and mitigation were introduced to urban development (Ishikawa, 2012). Hard infrastructure development, which was planned when Japan's economy was growing, continued to be implemented until recently. For example, the Kansai International Airport was built on an artificial island in Osaka Bay. Its planning started in the 1960s and it was opened in 1994 as a gateway to the western part of Japan, responding to the growing number of international passengers and problem of noise over the Osaka International Airport, which is in the urban area of Osaka. The risk of subsidence of the artificial island was acknowledged. According to the Kansai Airport, the average subsidence in 2020 since the opening in 1994 was 13.43m (including the subsidence of 9.82m during the period between the reclamation of the island and the opening) (Kansai Airports, n.d.). At the time of the 21st typhoon in 2018, the airport was inundated due to the storm surge and it suffered a large-scale blackout as the facility operation rooms in the basement were flooded (Kansai Airports, 2018). Aircraft noise became less of a problem during the 30 years of planning due to technological innovation. The necessity of developing an airport on the artificial island was agreed at the time of planning, but circumstances changed as time went by. Urban development projects take time to implement, and plans made a few decades ago may no longer be necessary or may need review when implemented.

Urban systems and management for enhanced disaster preparedness

The post-war urban infrastructure in Japan was based on the population and economic growth. The 'disaster prevention' measures were about developing/repairing dykes along rivers and coastal areas. Water management systems such as dams were also developed. These dams were important infrastructure to avoid floods through the control of water flow.

The trend of Japan's population decrease was recognised after 2000, in particular, since the Bureau of Statistics announced in 2005 that 'It seems that Japan has started to depopulate, with a 20,000 decrease compared with the previous year' and an actual decrease was observed after 2008 (Bureau of Statistics, 2012). While the population has decreased, the scale of natural hazards has increased. As mentioned, rather than 'disaster prevention,' 'disaster reduction' and 'mitigation' have become basic concepts for urban planning and infrastructure development. In addition, along with the increased risk of climate change, natural hazards other than earthquakes have been recognised as threats (Nakai, 2016). In fact, the impacts of floods and typhoons were disastrous in the 2010s.

After the North East Japan earthquake and tsunami of 2011, the Disaster Countermeasures Basic Act (implemented in 1961) was revised in 2013. The major change was to include the clear concept of the 'necessity of measures according to the risk level of hazards' (Ikuta, 2016). Ikuta (2016) pointed out that the existing measures assumed a mid-scale of hazard and had no framework to respond to larger ones such as the earthquake and tsunami in 2011. The lesson from 2011 was that infrastructure cannot save our lives. The revision of the Act applied the concept that even with a huge scale disaster, a combination of hard and soft infrastructure could mitigate the impact; the responsibility of residents to enhance preparedness was also specified (Ikuta, 2016).

After the 2011 disaster, it was suggested that urban areas should be redeveloped further from the coast, with flood prone areas in between the ocean and urban settlements. In many fishing villages which could not be moved inland, the relocation of residents to higher grounds (hills of the peninsulas in many cases) and raising the ground level were made mandatory. Even with these measures, residents are expected to evacuate as soon as a warning is issued (or they feel an earthquake). A combination of infrastructure maintenance/development and enhancing preparedness has become the norm since this disaster.

Kuroshio town, Kochi prefecture in Shikoku Island is predicted to have a more than 34m tsunami (highest among all areas of Japan) at the time of the Nankai Trough earthquake which is expected to occur in the near future. The town faces the Pacific Ocean. Evacuation towers up to 22m tall were developed in addition to upgrades of evacuation routes. Other facilities such as the storage of emergency goods, night lights and signage with information about evacuation routes were also provided (Kuroshio Town, 2016). The objective was to raise awareness amongst residents and prepare them for the next hazard. Evacuation drills using these towers and routes are conducted regularly. Also, a new factory was built to make tinned food, using locally caught seafood and vegetables, specifically for use in emergencies. Their tinned food menu is designed, where possible, to avoid ingredients which cause allergies.

Enhancing awareness and preparedness of residents is regarded as critical, and each local government is making efforts. Many governments updated 'hazard maps' after the 2011 disaster. The Ministry of Land, Infrastructure, Transport and Tourism developed a portal of hazard maps. Users can browse hazard maps for different disaster types on this portal.[5] A number of local governments have distributed printed versions of hazard maps to each household in their jurisdictions.

Local governments, no matter how big or how wealthy, have a duty to support their residents. Once residents are prepared, focus should move to people/areas that are especially vulnerable. The Tokyo Metropolitan Government published 'Disaster Preparedness Tokyo,' a disaster prevention booklet, in 2015. The booklet includes advice to residents on how they could enhance preparedness and how to respond based on a strong concept of 'self-help and mutual assistance' (Tokyo Metropolitan Government, 2020). The booklet is available in Japanese, English, Chinese and Korean.

In addition to hazard maps, the alert system has also been upgraded. 'L alert' was implemented in June 2011 by the Ministry of Internal Affairs and Communications. It is a system which sends information about natural hazards and evacuation advice/orders directly to residents' smartphones, radios, TVs and other devices using the internet. By 2019, all prefectures had adopted the system (Ministry of Internal Affairs and Communications, n.d.).

The focus of 'disaster prevention,' 'disaster reduction' and 'mitigation' are shifted from infrastructure development to reinforcing individuals' behaviour in preparing and acting to save their lives and help each other.

Notes

1 One of the 'Gokaido,' which was established in the Edo era, for traffic control. The Tokaido Corridor connects Tokyo, Nagoya, Kyoto and Osaka.

2 In Japan, a typhoon is usually called by the order of its emergence in each year – the first typhoon that developed after 1 January of each year is the 1st typhoon and so on.

3 *Shindo* is a unique seismic scale set out by the Japan Meteorological Agency, which is different from the scale of magnitude. *Shindo* ranges from 0–7 and 7 is the maximum. Seismic intensity meters are placed around 600 points across Japan where data is recorded. In the case of the Kumamoto earthquake, the first quake (14 April) was magnitude 6.5 and *Shindo* ranged from lower 5 to 7 and the second quake (16 April) was magnitude 7.3 and *Shindo* ranged from lower 5 to 7. At maximum *Shindo* 7, it is impossible to keep standing or move without crawling. People may be thrown through the air (www.jma.go.jp/jma/en/Activities/inttable.html).

4 This became the most critical accident of a nuclear power plant in the world after the Chernobyl disaster in 1986. As of March 2021, around 35,000 people are still yet to return to their homes in Fukushima (Reconstruction Agency, 2021).

5 https://disaportal.gsi.go.jp/ Accessed on 17 April 2022. Written in Japanese.

References

Architectural Institute of Japan. (2010). *About AIJ's decision with regard to 'disaster prevention in architecture' (1959) including the suggestion not use woods (Mokuzou kinshi wo fukumu Nihon Kenchiku Gakkai no Kenchikubosai ni Kansuruketsugi (1959) ni Tsuite).* www.aij.or.jp/jpn/databox/2010/20100726-1.htm (Accessed on 17 April 2022) [Written in Japanese].

Asano, J. (2012). A study on the first plan's idea of post-war reconstruction city plan and the relation with plans before and during world war II in local cities from cases of Kumamoto, Kochi, Okayama and Gifu. *Journal of Architecture and Planning, 77*(671), 27–36. [Written in Japanese].

Black, J. A. (2022). *A short history of transport in Japan from ancient times to the present.* Cambridge: Open Book Publishers.

Bureau of Statistics. (2012). *Tokei Today No.9.* www.stat.go.jp/info/today/009.html (Accessed on 17 April 2022) [Written in Japanese].

Honda, Y., Shimada, Y., & Kurosaki, Y. (1995). A study on influence of war damage on growth of cities. *School of Engineering, University of Fukui, Research Report, 43*(2) [Written in Japanese].

Ikuta, O. (2016). The structural problem and future prospects concerning the legal system of disaster prevention. *The Japanese Journal of Real Estate Sciences, 29*(4), 41–46 [Written in Japanese].

Ishikawa, M. (2012). Characteristics and target for the reconstruction from the Great East Japan Disaster. *Trends in the Sciences, 17*(11), 10–14 [Written in Japanese]. https://doi.org/10.5363/tits.17.11_10

Japan Society of Civil Engineers. (n.d.). *Proposal on earthquake resistance for civil engineering structures.* www.jsce.or.jp/committee/earth/index-e.html (Accessed on 17 April 2022).

Kansai Airports. (2018). *Disaster prevention measures (Saigai Taisaku ni Tsuite).* www.kansai-airports.co.jp/news/2018/2663/J181213_Disaster_prevention.pdf (Accessed on 17 April 2022) [Written in Japanese].

Kansai Airports. (n.d.). *About the subsidence (Chinka no Jyoukyou).* www.kansai-airports.co.jp/efforts/our-tech/kix/sink/sink3.html (Accessed on 17 April 2022) [Written in Japanese].

Kawakami, U. (1993). A study on the history of the Comprehensive National Development Plan from a viewpoint of the social backgrounds. *Historical Studies in Civil Engineering, 13*, 121–128. https://doi.org/10.2208/journalhs1990.13.121 [Written in Japanese].

Kawakami, U. (1995). A historical study on the transition of the national planning policy before the comprehensive national land development act. *Historical studies in civil engineering*, 15, 61–70. Written in Japanese. https://doi.org/10.2208/journalhs1990.15.61

Kuroshio Town. (2016). *Our preparation for the tsunami (Kuroshio Cho no Tsunami Bosai heno Torikumi)*. www.town.kuroshio.lg.jp/pb/cont/summit-japanese/6023 (Accessed on 15 April 2022) [Written in Japanese].

Maeda, N., Inoue, O., Takemura, Y., & Sanaka, T. (1995). Development system of infrastructure in Japan – A study for future system in comparison with some of U.S. systems. *Journal of Construction Management, 3*, 43–58. https://doi.org/10.2208/procm.3.43 [Written in Japanese].

Ministry of Internal Affairs and Communications. (n.d.). *The promotion of L alert (L alert Saigai Zyouhou Kyouyuu Sisutemu no Fukyu Sokushin)*. www.soumu.go.jp/menu_seisaku/ictseisaku/ictriyou/02ryutsu06_03000032.html (Accessed on 15 April 2022) [Written in Japanese].

Ministry of Land, Infrastructure, Transport and Tourism. (1998). *The 5th Comprehensive National Development Plan*. www.mlit.go.jp/kokudokeikaku/zs5-e/index.html (Accessed on 20 November 2020).

Nakai, N. (2016). Disaster prevention and mitigation in the post East Japan Great Earthquake era. *The Japanese Journal of Real Estate Sciences, 29*(4), 30 [Written in Japanese].

Nakanishi, H., & Kurauchi, F. (2021). Japan's Linear Megalopolis, Shinkansen high-speed rail as the spine of a 60-year mega-region evolution'. In M. Neuman & W. Zonneveld (Eds.), *The Routledge handbook for regional design*. New York: Routledge.

Reconstruction Agency. (2021). *Road to recovery and prospects March 2021*. www.reconstruction.go.jp/topics/main-cat1/sub-cat1-1/2021.3_mchinori.pdf (Accessed on 4 March 2022) [Written in Japanese].

Sorensen, A. (2002). *The making of urban Japan cities and planning from Edo to the twenty first century*. London: Routledge.

Tokyo Metropolitan Government. (2020). *The disaster prevention booklet 'Disaster Preparedness Tokyo*. https://translation2.j-server.com/LUCAITBSAI/ns/tl.cgi/www.bousai.metro.tokyo.lg.jp/1002147/1007120.html?SLANG=ja&TLANG=en&XMODE=0&XPARAM=q,&XCHARSET=UTF-8&XPORG=,&XJSID=0 (Accessed on 15 April 2022).

Yada, T. (2014). On the national land development plans by the Japanese government since 1950 *Sengo kokudo keikaku sakutei no kozu Shimokobe shogen kara yomitoku. Association of Economic Geographers Annals, 60*(2), 47–63 [Written in Japanese].

Yamada, H. (1994). Economic growth, urbanization and regional policy in post-war Japan *Sengo no keizaiseichou, toshika to kokudo seisaku. Society of Civil Engineers Journal of Infrastructure Planning and Management, 494*(IV-24), 1–12 [Written in Japanese].

3 Social capital

Community responses to natural hazards

Transition of Japanese society

In the past, most Japanese communities were based on an agricultural/farming lifecycle. Members of the same village co-operated and co-developed the irrigation system and shared agricultural infrastructure resources (including sharing labour to maintain these). As now, the most hazardous events for agriculture-based communities were droughts, floods and typhoons. In autumn, they celebrated the harvest together as a form of *'matsuri'*[1] or *'Aki matsuri'* (autumn festival), appreciating mother nature and thanking god for bringing the harvest without serious natural hazards. They also organised seasonal events together. Residents protected local shrines, which they regarded as the home of the god of Shinto. They protected them as sacred places and organised seasonal events (such as *Matsuri*) there. Life revolved around this agriculture-based society, where residents provided 'mutual help.' People faithfully followed the oral traditions shared by ancestors. They developed villages only on lands that had survived past natural hazards and only used architectural styles that had proved resilient (Terada, 2011).

The *'gonin-gumi'* system (established during the reign of Tokugawa Government 1603–1867) is the origin of the neighbourhood association which used to help residents to develop and share knowledge in dealing with natural hazards (Braibanti, 1948; Nakanishi & Black, 2018) in agriculture-based society. The *'gonin-gumi'* was also a system by which residents monitored each other as they shared the responsibilities of paying taxes and preventing crimes. The principle of *'gonin-gumi'* was diminished by the modernisation which was implemented after the commencement of Meiji era (1867). During the period of modernisation, local governments started to manage local infrastructure. However, a quasi-feudal societal system remained in many ways (Lockwood, 1954). After World War II, the neighbourhood association became independent voluntary bodies organised by residents (Nakanishi & Black, 2018).[2] At the same time, the strong cooperative system was

DOI: 10.4324/9781003150190-3

adopted by many Japanese companies in the age of rapid economic growth, where workers shared long working hours and family activities together (Koukami, 2009). Japan's growth was supported by this co-operative system, which was based on lifelong employment.[3]

The population of rural agriculture communities has been declining since the 1960s and the trend is still continuing, along with an increase in the proportion of older people in such areas (Ministry of Agriculture, Forestry and Fisheries, 2015). This has resulted in the decline of the traditional 'mutual help' system in rural areas. In addition, the declining number of young people is calamitous because there are not enough to assist older people at a time of natural hazard.

'*Seken*' is also another form of community in Japan (Abe, 1995). It has a significant impact on how people behave by setting certain norms for people who belong to '*seken*.' It connects individuals with strong ties and Japanese people prioritise '*seken*' above their individual principles (Abe, 1995). This is revealed in many forms. '*Seken*' is an exclusive and tight-knit community which is similar to village-based communities in the pre-modern era. Working for their village to prevent and prepare for natural hazards is a rule of '*seken*' (Koukami, 2009). Anyone who does not follow the rules is excluded from the village (this is called '*Mura hachibu*'). The invisible rule of '*seken*' is effective at a time of disaster because members behave relatively rationally under the norm of '*seken*.' As previously mentioned, the '*gonin-gumi*' system disappeared from society. However, the strong norm of '*seken*' still remains in Japanese society (for example, almost all people in Japan wore masks during the COVID-19 outbreak without any mandatory measures of local governments. This is because of '*seken*').

Post-war societal change is shown in Figure 3.1. Japan's post-war economic policies established the basis of a 'middle-class nation' along with the nuclearisation of families (Fujita, 2011; Ronald & Hirayama, 2009). Household patterns increasingly revolved around a standard male breadwinner and female homemaker model and the formation of nuclear urban families (Ronald & Hirayama, 2009). The rise of women's education levels and workforce participation triggered delayed marriage and lower birth rates from 1975 onward (Jones, 2007).

However, the Japanese labour market continued to make a clear distinction between jobs for women (part-time, non-career) and those for men (full-time, long hours with promotion and career advancement) (Rindfuss et al., 2004). Compared with Western societies, marriage in Japan is more strictly linked with childbearing, childrearing and caring for elderly parents. The prevailing situation before the Equal Employment Opportunity Law enacted in 1987 was that employed women quit after marriage. The Basic Law for a Gender-equal Society was enacted in 1999 to promote gender equality both in the workplace and at home. However, household tasks within marriage are still extremely gender segregated, with the burden overwhelmingly on the wife.

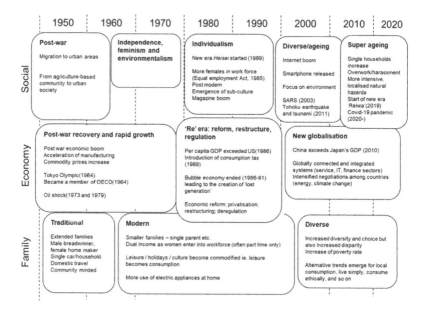

Figure 3.1 Transition of Japanese society, economy and family

Source: (original of the author)

In contrast, professionals (generally male) work long hours in a high-demand corporate culture (Bachika et al., 2011; Tsai et al., 2016). Japanese husbands employed full-time work 49 or more hours a week and one in five works 60 hours or more, much longer than those in Western countries. This causes a significant time pressure on employed wives both in the household and workplace, while their husbands make a limited contribution to chores and childrearing (Tsuya et al., 2005). Government policies to support childcare and care for elderly parents are still not sufficient (Prime Minister of Japan and His Cabinet, 2017). Japanese couples have almost no choice but to have less or no children or delay childbearing until they have a management role with flexible work arrangements or enough income to outsource support at their own cost.

Before the bubble economy of the 1980s, many people could earn enough money to live and save for the future. Also, some people could move to a higher class (for example, from the labour class to the elite class). The employment rate of young people was stable, and they could develop a financial foundation to raise a family. Purchasing a home was a milestone for young nuclear families in the 'all middle-class' society of Japan. Likewise, buying a car became an aspiration for young people and peaked in the 1980s. However, for current young adults, home and car ownership are no longer feasible (Hirayama, 2010; Japan Automobile Manufacturers Association, 2014; Kuhnimhof et al., 2012), partly due to economic concerns.

Prolonged deflation, along with the deregulation of the labour market, caused a dramatic growth in precarious employment in Japan (Osawa et al., 2013). Since the 1990s, young people are more likely to be engaged in casual jobs with the disadvantaged conditions[4] of low pay and little job security, with fewer full-time professional jobs available to them. More single young adults are living with their parents, with little contributions to household expenses (Retherford et al., 2001) and further delayed marriage. The proportion of unmarried young adults has changed dramatically: 95.0% (male, 20–24 years old) and 91.4% (female, 20–24 years old), 72.7% (male, 25–29 years old) and 61.3 % (female, 25–29 years old), 47.1% (male, 30–34 years old) and 34.6 % (female, 30–34 years old) in 2015, compared with 90.1%, 46.5% and 11.7% (average) in 1970 respectively (Ministry of Health Labour and Welfare, 2020). In fact, many young people still aspire to mainstream traditional lifestyles[5] but have to negotiate more insecure socioeconomic conditions compared with their predecessors (Ronald & Hirayama, 2009). On the other hand, the percentage of single persons living with parents is extremely high compared with Western countries – 72.2% among men and 78.2% among women in 2015 (National Institute of Population and Social Security Research, 2016), reflecting the difficult situations faced by young adults.

The author had an opportunity to discuss life prospects and concerns with young adults (in their 20s and 30s) living in the Tokyo metropolitan area and surrounding cities in September–November 2016. Participants (23) were recruited through 'purposive' and 'snowballing' sampling techniques by using authors' professional networks and social network services. The majority of the participants worked full-time after finishing high school, vocational school, undergraduate or postgraduate degrees. The part-time worker, casual worker and homemaker were all females.

Participants showed their concerns about financial security.

> '*I am concerned about my pension. I am not sure if we will get enough pension.*'
> '*I am not sure if I will have enough income to achieve my preferred life course.*'

Unlike previous generations who worked long hours, they prioritise a good balance of work and life.

> '*With my first job, I worked in weekends and by midnight every day. I had no time to relax. My current job is better because I have my own time.*'
> '*I think balance is important. I want to prioritise my family.*'

They did not show much interest in owning a house or a car.

> '*I don't need to own a car as far as I am living in Tokyo. Public transport is sufficient. If I need, I will rent a car.*'
> '*If we are having one more child, the place we are currently renting will become too small . . . a brand-new house is not affordable for us here. Indeed we really don't need a brand-new house.*'

These are just examples from a small number of interviewees. However, these narratives demonstrate that, compared to previous generations who benefited from economic growth and hard work, current young adults have many concerns about financial security and their work life balance.

As previously mentioned, even with the implementation of the Equal Employment Opportunity Law, the issue of the clear distinction between jobs for women and those for men, and the associated pay gap, has not been resolved. According to the most recent survey from the Ministry of Health, Labour and Welfare, which was conducted in 2016, the number of households headed by a single parent was 12,320,000 (female parent) and 1,870,000 (male parent) (Ministry of Health, Labour and Welfare, 2017). Divorce (more than 75%) and bereavement are the main causes. The total number of single parent households has decreased since the previous survey in 2012. However, the issue here is the financial vulnerability of female-parent households. More than 81% of female parents had jobs, but 43.8% worked part time, followed by full time (44.2%), whilst 68.2% of their male counterparts had full time jobs, followed by self-employed (18.2%) and part time (6.4%). Accordingly, the gap in their annual income – 2430,000 yen (21,300 USD[6]) for females and 4,200,000 yen (36,800 USD) for males – is significant. This is contributing to a widening inequality between socioeconomic groups in Japan (see details in Chapter 7).

Social capital and its role in disaster responses and recovery – evidence from cases

Agriculture based communities have nurtured social capital historically. As mentioned previously, sharing resources and celebrating harvest together contributed to developing reciprocity and tight-knit communities. In this pre-modern society, 'mutual help' was systemised. In particular, in *mura* (village) society, human relationships were based on the identification and solidarity of living in the same place, based on the characteristics of Japanese people who were (and still are) likely to place more importance on the harmony of the group than preferences/needs of individuals (Onda, 2013).

Tight-knit communities tend to have strong social capital. Social capital is believed to further facilitate the recovery of affected communities more than other factors (Aldrich, 2012). Aldrich (2012)[7] discussed higher solidarity seen through high participation in civic activities and the strong connection between residents, which contributed to better recovery outcomes in examining cases of the Tokyo earthquake 1923 and the Kobe earthquake 1995. Relationships with neighbours were regarded as important in solving housing and rebuilding issues. Neighbourhoods in which residents were less connected and had lower levels of trust and suffered more from the impact of the disaster in the case of the Kobe earthquake 1995 (Aldrich, 2012). Aldrich's argument has been supported by other researchers. For example, Nakagawa and Shaw (2004) discussed that the case of the Kobe earthquake showed that communities with social capital, along with residents' efforts and leadership brought mutual benefit to severely affected communities and facilitated successful rehabilitation. Olshansky et al. (2006) reported that citizen '*machizukuri*'[8] organisations played critical roles in the recovery of neighbourhoods after the Kobe earthquake. They liaised with residents and city government to find mutual benefits.

Shaw (2014) evaluated that the Kobe earthquake was a turning point for community-based approaches to recovery in Japan, discussing a new dimension of civil society which emerged through recovery programs. In fact, a system involving 'disaster volunteers' who engage in activities with a long-term perspective (even after the immediate rescue/relief period), a framework to organise these volunteers (e.g., as a form of non-profit organisation) and networking them emerged after the Kobe earthquake (Suzuki et al., 2003). A national network of volunteer organisations such as the Nippon Volunteer Network Active in Disaster (NVNAD) was established. These volunteers and non-profit organisations (NPOs) gained experience and greatly contributed in the aftermath of the North East Japan earthquake and tsunami in 2011. In addition to the cleaning of debris and delivery of emergency goods, supporting vulnerable people (e.g., older people) in the process of recovery was revealed to be a critical role of these volunteer organisations (Nakajima et al., 2012).

The networks and strong ties of Japanese communities were revealed and widely broadcast after the North East Japan earthquake and tsunami in 2011. International media reported that Japanese people in the affected communities were sharing food and petrol with neighbours and remaining calm and polite despite long queues at the shops (for example, ABC, 2011).

Aldrich (2019) discussed that communities where residents had strong ties worked together to '*push past bureaucratic obstacles and support innovative leadership*,' whilst less connected communities suffered in the recovery process. For instance, the fishing villages that were affected by the tsunami waves are very tight-knit. They have a well nurtured community, which made their decision making to relocate to higher grounds conflict free (Nakazawa, 2013).

Figure 3.2 Dancing demonstration at Matsuri
Source: (taken by the author in October, 2016)

Social connections can help survivors make positive choices (Aldrich, 2019). Social capital strengthening or building programs have been lifesavers for many who would otherwise be isolated (Aldrich, 2019). In fact, the author listened to stories from many survivors of the tsunami. Their feelings are consistent with this. Some of the survivors told the author that volunteer people who came from outside the affected area facilitated the conversation with residents from different generations. In particular young people (in their 20s and 30s) encouraged older people to work together for recovery (Blackman et al., 2017). The traditional events such as *matsuri* were a good opportunity for residents to get together, prepare food and appreciate their achievements after the disaster (Figures 3.2 and 3.3).

Figure 3.3 A float parading in town at Matsuri
Source: (taken by the author in October, 2016)

There are also organisations that victims established after the disaster to help each other and support the recovery of local areas. The author met a couple who are the leaders of one of the organisations of this kind. The couple lost their three children in the tsunami. They were devastated and did not have any hope for the future just after the disaster. However, they were buoyed by the support of people at their shelter and established a volunteer organisation called 'Team Watahoi.' Their aim is to support affected people, in particular, children who lost their parents in the tsunami. Figure 3.4 shows a playground which was built on the ground where the couple's house was before the disaster. There is a container house where members do their activities next to the playground. They organise events with local people here.

Figure 3.4 Base of 'Team Watahoi' and playground
Source: (taken by the author in July, 2019)

The social capital of communities established in the pre-modern era diminished as new people migrated and built new neighbourhoods. However, new social networks have been built. In the aftermath of disaster, people relocate from place to place (Nakanishi & Black, 2016). They help each other in the process of recovery and nurture trust. In disaster prone areas, new networks and social capital emerge over time.

Contemporary challenges of Japanese society

In the current individualistic Japanese society, many people do not belong to neighbourhood associations. People tend to be more self-involved, compared with the pre-modernisation era (Onda, 2013). Neighbourhood associations played pivotal roles in providing information that contributed to the management of temporary housing and the reconstruction process in post mega disaster recovery such as the Kobe earthquake (Aldrich, 2012; Ueda & Shaw, 2016).

Also, in North East Japan, where there are tight-knit communities, people helped each other with neighbours. The narratives that follow are quoted from the book *Surviving the 2011 Tsunami: 100 Testimonies of Ishinomaki Area Survivors of the Great East Japan Earthquake* (Editorial Office of the Ishinomaki Kahoku A daily Newspaper of Sanriku Kahoku Shimpo, 2014).[9]

> '*After seeing my parents get out of the house, my thoughts turned to helping the elderly man living next door to us and evacuating with him.*' (p. 70)
>
> '*I got the emergency food, lights and heaters ready for my family and next-door neighbour.*' (p. 101)
>
> '*I learned that a bedridden woman was still in her house 100 metres away. Four of us men set out to rescue her. We rolled her up in the futon bedding she was resting in, tied a rope around it, and carried her to a Buddhist temple on higher ground.*' (p. 178–179)
>
> '*When I was about to give up hope, a boat with a man on it approached me, and I was hauled up onto the boat. I was frozen, and I couldn't do anything but cling to the owner of the boat.*' (p. 221)
>
> '*the second floor of their house was intact, and the couple said, "You're welcome to use whatever there is up there" . . . we took them up on the offer and the firefighter went out to get such things as blankets and clothes . . . we were fortunate to have a hot water pot as well, and we could drink warm water . . . the woman who was suffering from a low body temperature survived.*' (p. 224)

However, in most Japanese communities, this is not happening, as many people don't know their neighbours well and don't have a strong network in the neighbourhood (see Chapter 4). In addition to scarce interaction between neighbours, even accelerating ageing poses a big challenge at the time of natural hazards. Older people generally prefer to stay home by frequently conducting 'vertical evacuation' (that is, moving upstairs within a building), rather than evacuating elsewhere. With assistance from neighbours and the community, older people may be more inclined to evacuate (Ishii & Nakamura, 2018; Katada et al., 2002).

In Japan, it is expected that the proportion of older people (65 years old and above) will be 33.3% in 2036 (up 6.7% from 26.6% in 2015) and it will be 38.4% in 2065, which means 1 out of 2.6 people will be over 65 years old (National Institute of Population and Social Security Research, 2017). In addition, instances of older people who are living alone are increasing. It is expected that the proportion of older males living alone (75 years old and above) will increase from 12.8% (2015) to 16.1% by 2030 and the proportion of older females living alone (75 years old and above) will increase from 25.6% (2015) to 26.1% by 2030 (National Institute of Population and Social Security Research, 2018). Neighbourhood association leaders are already struggling to help older people, even in the current situation. Older people hesitate to drive when it is raining heavily (e.g., during floods and typhoons) (Nakanishi et al., 2019). In pre-modern society or in tight-knit communities, neighbours used to help, but this is not realistic in many current Japanese communities. Ideally, qualified people should be dispatched to help older people to get ready and evacuate, but if the proportion of older people keeps growing, this will be more difficult in the future. It is expected that as technology advances, autonomous cars could be used to collect older people and bring them to shelters. But it may take a while until this measure can be applied practically.

The problem is not just with older people. The number of single-mother households has also increased from 790,000 (1993) to 1,230,000 (2016) (Gender Equality Bureau, Cabinet Office, 2019). These households also need assistance as they are often not well connected with neighbours and need help in bringing young children and emergency goods to shelters.

Immigrant households also need assistance. The number of immigrants living in Japan has been increasing. Even during the short period between 2017 and 2019, the number increased to 2,933,137 from 2,561,848 (Statistics Bureau of Japan, 2021). This includes both high-skilled and low-skilled workers whose numbers have steadily increased as the result of the recent shift in policy (Kobayashi, 2018). Not only the number but also the backgrounds of immigrants have become more diversified. In addition, before COVID-19, inbound tourism steadily continued to thrive since 2012, reaching approximately 19 million as of July 2018 with an 13.9 % average increase from the preceding year (Japanese National Tourism Organisation, 2018).

'I was trembling with fear, due to lack of information. I have never experienced earthquakes in my own country.'

This is a comment of a tourist affected by an earthquake in June 2018. The Western Japan flood of 2018 (Chapter 6) revealed that the Hiroshima, Okayama and Ehime prefectural governments did not have figures identifying how many non-Japanese residents had sought shelter at evacuation centres set up by local governments (The Japan Times, 2018).

As the depopulation and ageing accelerates, it is expected that immigrant workers are going to play a key role in the Japanese labour market. However, they are often not considered as part of communities and are considerably disadvantaged in coping with disasters (Kobayashi & Nakanishi, 2017). For long-term foreign residents, disaster drills are significant. Even those with some command of the Japanese language with access to information have experienced fear, which impinges on their disaster coping ability. Disaster drills would provide them with multiple tools, in addition to enhancing their knowledge. It would connect them to Japanese local communities and nurture a sense of locality, which would equip foreign residents with the preparedness to make an educated and informed judgement, even when disasters exceed predictions.

Notes

1 'Matsuri' is organised with various objectives and forms. In agricultural areas, it is often organised to pray for a good harvest, no natural hazards (such as drought and floods) and to appreciate the harvest. Matsuri involves dancing with traditional music, parading floats etc.
2 'Tonari gumi' which was implemented during the era of the Second World War followed the system of 'gonin-gumi' but it was abolished in 1947.
3 This somewhat 'social and economic safe' system was broken after the long recession which started in the 1990s.
4 Nonregular workers comprised 19.1% of the labour force in 1989 and increased to 38.3% by 2019. Female nonregular workers were 56.0% whilst male non regular workers were 22.9% in 2019 (Ministry of Health, Labour and Welfare, 2020).
5 The proportion of never-married persons who intend to marry someday is high – 85.7 % for men and 89.3% for women (National Institute of Population and Social Security Research, 2016).
6 Based on a currency exchange rate on 14 January 2022.
7 Aldrich measured social capital through the propensity to participate in civic affairs such as voting and mobilising for public events for the case of the Tokyo earthquake 1923. In terms of the Kobe earthquake in 1995, time series cross-sectional data as the number of new neighbourhood-level NPOs created per capita was used.
8 Means town planning. 'Machidukuri' organisations are often non-profit and operated by local residents with the support of local governments, business and experts.
9 The author was a member of the editorial team.

References

ABC. (2011). *Japanese, waiting in line for hours, follow social order after quake. Experts say Japanese value hierarchy and helping spirit, but are fatalists.* https://abcnews.go.com/Health/japan-victims-show-resilience-earthquake-tsunami-sign-sense/story?id=13135355 (Accessed on 9 April 2022).

Abe, K. (1995). *What is Seken?* (*Seken to ha nanika*). Tokyo, Japan: Kodansha Ltd (the translation of the title is made by the author) [Written in Japanese].

Aldrich, D. P. (2012). *Building resilience: Social capital in post-disaster recovery.* Chicago, IL: University of Chicago Press.

Aldrich, D. P. (2019). *Black wave: How networks and governance shaped Japan's 3/11 disasters.* Chicago, IL: University of Chicago Press.

Bachika, R., Schulz, M. S., & North, S. (2011). Deadly virtues: Inner-worldly asceticism and karôshi in Japan. *Current Sociology, 59*, 146–159. https://doi.org/10.1177/0011392110391145.

Blackman, D., Nakanishi, H., & Benson, A. M. (2017). Disaster resilience as a complex problem: Why linearity is not applicable for long-term recovery.

Technological Forecasting and Social Change, 121, 89–98. https://doi. org/10.1016/j.techfore.2016.09.018

Braibanti, R. J. D. (1948). Neighborhood associations in Japan and their democratic potentialities. *The Far Eastern Quarterly, 7*(2), 136–164. https://doi. org/10.2307/2048859

Editorial Office of the Ishinomaki Kahoku a Daily Newspaper of Sanriku Kahoku Shimpo. (2014). *Surviving the 2011 tsunami: 100 Testimonies of Ishinomaki area survivors of the great East Japan Earthquake*. Tokyo, Japan: Junposha Publishing Co., Ltd.

Fujita, K. (2011). Financial crises, Japan's state regime shift, and Tokyo's urban policy. *Environment and Planning A: Economy and Space, 43*(2), 307–327. https:// doi.org/10.1068/a43111

Gender Equality Bureau, Cabinet Office. (2019). *The white paper on gender equality 2019*. Tokyo, Japan: Ministry of Internal Affairs and Communications, The Government of Japan [Written in Japanese].

Hirayama, Y. (2010). The role of home ownership in Japan's aged society. *Journal of Housing and the Built Environment, 25*, 175–191. https://doi.org/10.1007/ s10901-010-9183-8

Ishii, R., & Nakamura, H. (2018). Evacuation behaviors of elderly people and assisting behaviors of care managers in the event of an earthquake-induced fire or large-scale flood. *Journal of the City Planning Institute of Japan, 3*(53), 875–880. https://doi.org/10.11361/journalcpij.53.875 [Written in Japanese].

Japan Automobile Manufacturers Association. (2014). Young people and car (Wakamono to Kuruma). *Jamagazine, 48* (the translation of the title is made by the author) [Written in Japanese].

Japanese National Tourism Organisation. (2018). *Press release*. www.jnto.go.jp/jpn/ statistics/data_info_listing/pdf/180815_monthly.pdf (Accessed on 9 April 2022) [Written in Japanese].

Jones, G. W. (2007). Delayed marriage and very low fertility in Pacific Asia. *Population and Development Review, 33*, 453–478. https://doi.org/10.1111/ j.1728-4457.2007.00180.x

Katada, T., Yamaguchi, H., & Kanzawa, H. (2002). Research on the evacuation activities of elderly and the social support for elderly during river flood disasters. *Journal of Japanese Association for an Inclusive Society, 4*(1), 17–26 [Written in Japanese].

Kobayashi, H. Y., & Nakanishi, H. (2017). Involvement of immigrants in community planning for disaster resilience: A prospect and paradigm. *Urban Perspective Quality Design Institute Bulletin, 2*, 16–23.

Kobayashi, Y. H. (2018). From non-immigrant country to de facto immigrant country: Recent shifts in Japanese immigration policy. In N. Farrelly (Ed.), *People movement* (pp. 57–61). Canberra: ANU College of Asia and Pacific.

Koukami, S. (2009). '*Air' and 'Seken' ('Kuuki' to 'Seken')*. Tokyo, Japan: Kodansha Ltd (the translation of the title is made by the author) [Written in Japanese].

Kuhnimhof, T., Armoogum, J., Buehler, R., Dargay, J., Denstadili, J. M., & Yamamoto, T. (2012). Men shape a downward trend in car use among young adults – Evidence from six industrialized countries. *Transport Reviews, 32*, 761–779. https://doi.org/10.1080/01441647.2012.736426

Lockwood, W. W. (1954). *The economic development of Japan growth and structural change 1868–1938.* Princeton, NJ: Princeton University Press.

Ministry of Agriculture, Forestry and Fisheries. (2015). *White paper on food, agriculture and rural areas.* Tokyo, Japan: The Government of Japan [Written in Japanese].

Ministry of Health, Labour and Welfare. (2017). *Summary of results of national single parent household survey 2016.* Tokyo, Japan: The Government of Japan [Written in Japanese].

Ministry of Health, Labour and Welfare. (2020). *White paper 2020.* Tokyo, Japan: The Government of Japan [Written in Japanese].

Nakagawa, Y., & Shaw, R. (2004). Social capital: A missing link to disaster recovery. *International Journal of Mass Emergencies and Disasters, 22*(1), 5–34.

Nakajima, M., Shiota, H., & Kawazoe, S. (2012). The contribution of local NPO in reducing the disparity of reconstruction support after the Great East Japan Earthquake. *Journal of Rural Planning Association, 31*(3), 498–502 [Written in Japanese].

Nakanishi, H., & Black, J. (2016). Residential relocation, school relocation and children's transport: The effect of the Great East Japan Earthquake and Tsunami 2011. *International Journal of Disaster Risk Reduction, 18,* 232–243. https://doi.org/10.1016/j.ijdrr.2016.07.006

Nakanishi, H., & Black, J. (2018). Implicit and explicit knowledge in flood evacuations with a case study of Takamatsu, Japan. *International Journal of Disaster Risk Reduction, 28,* 788–797. https://doi.org/10.1016/j.ijdrr.2018.02.008

Nakanishi, H., Black, J., & Suenaga, Y. (2019). Investigating the flood evacuation behaviour of older people: A case study of a rural town in Japan. *Research in Transportation Business & Management, 30,* 100376. https://doi.org/10.1016/j.rtbm.2019.100376

Nakazawa, H. (2013). Resilience and social care two years after the Great East Japan Earthquake. *The Annual Review of Sociology, 26,* 17–27. https://doi.org/10.5690/kantoh.2013.17 [Written in Japanese].

National Institute of Population and Social Security Research. (2016). *The fifteenth Japanese National Fertility Survey in 2015, marriage process and fertility of married couples attitudes toward marriage and family among Japanese Singles, highlights of the survey results on married couples/singles.* Tokyo, Japan: Ministry of Health, Labour and Welfare of Japan [Written in Japanese].

National Institute of Population and Social Security Research. (2017). *Population projections for Japan.* Tokyo, Japan: Ministry of Health, Labour and Welfare of Japan [Written in Japanese].

National Institute of Population and Social Security Research. (2018). *Projection of household numbers in Japan.* Tokyo, Japan: Ministry of Health, Labour and Welfare of Japan [Written in Japanese].

Olshansky, R. B., Johnson, L. A., & Topping, K. C. (2006). Rebuilding communities following disaster: Lessons from Kobe and Los Angeles. *Built Environment, 32*(4), 354–374. www.jstor.org/stable/23289510 (Accessed on 9 April 2022).

Onda, M. (2013). Mutual help networks and social transformation in Japan. *American Journal of Economics and Sociology, 72*(3), 531–564. www.jstor.org/stable/23526051 (Accessed on 9 April 2022).

Osawa, M., Kim, M. J., & Kingston, J. (2013). Precarious work in Japan. *American Behavioral Scientist, 57*(3), 309–334. https://doi.org/10.1177/0002764212466240

Prime Minister of Japan and His Cabinet. (2017). *The action plan for the realization of work style reform (Provisional)*. Tokyo, Japan: The Government of Japan [Written in Japanese].

Retherford, R. D., Ogawa, N., & Matsukura, R. (2001). Late marriage and less marriage in Japan. *Population and Development Review, 27*, 65–102. https://doi.org/10.1111/j.1728-4457.2001.00065.x

Rindfuss, R. R., Bumpass, L. L., Choe, M. K., et al. (2004). Social networks and family change in Japan. *American Sociological Review, 69*(6), 838–861. www.jstor.org/stable/3593045 (Accessed on 9 April 2022).

Ronald, R., & Hirayama, Y. (2009). Home alone: The individualization of young, urban Japanese singles. *Environment and Planning A: Economy and Space, 41*(12), 2836–2854. https://doi.org/10.1068/a41119

Shaw, R. (2014). Kobe earthquake: turning point of community-based risk reduction in Japan. In: Shaw, R. (eds) Community Practices for Disaster Risk Reduction in Japan. *Disaster Risk Reduction*. Tokyo, Japan: Springer. https://doi.org/10.1007/978-4-431-54246-9_2

Suzuki, I., Suga, M., & Atsumi, T. (2003). Disaster volunteers in Japan: A historical review and the current movement since the 1995 Kobe earthquake. *The Japanese Journal of Experimental Social Psychology, 42*(2), 166–186. https://doi.org/10.2130/jjesp.42.166 [Written in Japanese]

Statistics Bureau of Japan. (2021). *Statistics of Japan 2021*. Tokyo, Japan: Ministry of Internal Affairs and Communications of Japan [Written in Japanese].

Terada, T. (2011). Natural hazard and Japanese people. In T. Yamaori (Ed.), *Tensai to Nihonjin*. Tokyo, Japan: Kadokawa (the translation of the title is made by the author) [Written in Japanese].

The Japan Times. (2018). *No foreign nationals listed among dead in western Japan rain disasters, survey of prefectures shows 13 July 2018*. www.japantimes.co.jp/news/2018/07/13/national/no-foreign-nationals-listed-among-dead-western-japan-rain-disasters-survey-prefectures-shows/#.W4yTsoVOI5F (Accessed on 28 January 2022).

Tsai, M. C., Nitta, M., Kim, S. W., & Wang, W. (2016). Working overtime in East Asia: Convergence or divergence? *Journal of Contemporary Asia, 46*(4), 700–722. https://doi.org/10.1080/00472336.2016.1144778

Tsuya, N. O., Bumpass, L. L., Choe, M. K., & Rindfuss, R. R. (2005). Is the gender division of labour changing in Japan? *Asian Population Studies, 1*(1), 47–67. https://doi.org/10.1080/17441730500125805

Ueda, Y., & Shaw, R. (2016). Managing and bridging communities in temporary housing: Case of the Great East Japan Earthquake and Tsunami in Kesennuma City, Japan. *Natural Hazards, 80*(1), 567–587. https://doi.org/10.1007/s11069-015-1984-3

4 Typhoon nation

Lessons of 2004

The year 2004 is remembered as a year of typhoons. The first typhoon was observed in April and following this, typhoons continued to be reported until December, amounting to 29 typhoons in total.[1] Of the 29 typhoons, 10 landed on Japan. In particular, the 16th, 21st and 23rd typhoons had a significant impact as summarised in Chapter 2.

In this chapter, the impact and the responses to these typhoons in Kagawa prefecture and its capital city of Takamatsu, are discussed. Historically, the city has often been affected by the impact of typhoons (Nakanishi & Black, 2018). The natural hazards that have been most damaging to the Takamatsu area have been typhoons and associated storm surges, floods and landslides. The impact of these events has been mitigated over time by upgrades to infrastructure and civil engineering technology. However, the risk of natural hazards in the future is still expected to be high. The city's disaster management authority has been strengthening its defences against future hazards, in particular for the Nankai Trough earthquake[2] that is expected to occur soon. Even in this inland sea area, tsunamis are expected, which residents have not experienced before. The impact of storm surges accompanying big typhoons should also not be under-estimated, even if residents have some experience with these; a record breaking storm surge might happen due to the changes in the environment.

The location of Takamatsu is shown in Figure 4.1. It is located in the Seto Inland Sea National Park area. Kagawa prefecture is known as the driest prefecture in Japan, with a subtropical climate. Although, historically, the area has suffered from floods caused by typhoons, drought has been the major concern for many residents. For this reason, many irrigation ponds were developed to secure water for agriculture (Kihara et al., 2012).

A wake-up call: 16th typhoon (2004)

The 16th typhoon of 2004 (also known as Typhoon Chaba 2004) was created in mid-August when the tidal level was at its highest (called the summer tide in Japan). The typhoon came close to the Seto Inland Sea during

DOI: 10.4324/9781003150190-4

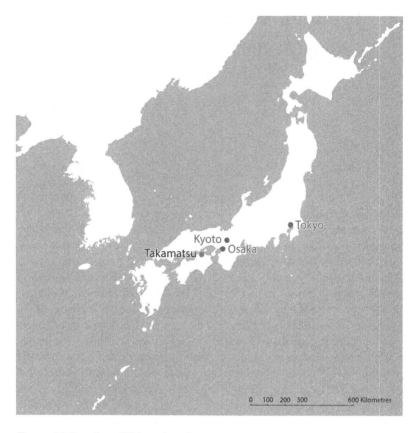

Figure 4.1 Location of Takamatsu-city

high-tide time on 30 August. The Takamatsu local meteorological observatory issued a storm surge warning at 15:50, with an expected tidal level of 220cm (Kagawa University, 2004). However, this was exceeded and the level reached 246–56 cm, which has become the historical record.[3] The inundation of the Takamatsu city centre started around 21:30 before the expected high tide time of 23:59. Other cities and towns in Kagawa were also inundated until around 22:00. In Takamatsu, the inundation continued until around 1:30 (Figure 4.2). The water receded in the morning, except for one part of the city (Kagawa University, 2004).

Due to the storm surge, more than 15,000 houses were flooded and 35 city facilities were damaged. It has been noted that the response of the city of Takamatsu was late. The headquarters for disaster management was only organised after the inundation started (Nakanishi & Black, 2018).

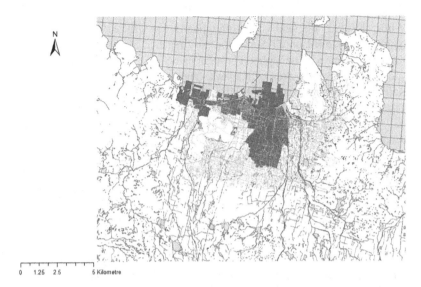

Figure 4.2 Flooded neighbourhoods of Takamatsu city

Source: (map made by the author)

Figure 4.3 Photo of flooded neighbourhood

Source: (provided by a resident)

Impact of landslides: the 21st typhoon (2004)

Whilst the area affected by the 16th typhoon was still recovering, the 21st typhoon developed on 21 September and reached Shikoku Island, where Kagawa is located. The typhoon brought heavy rain, causing massive landslides in the western area of Kagawa. The landslides damaged the Japan Railway train tracks, agricultural land, fruit farms and irrigation ponds. The debris flow that followed the landslide significantly impacted residential areas. This debris flow occurred due to the disintegration of the valley head and hillslope. This caused a torrent of detritus covering fruits farms on the hillslopes (Kagawa University, 2004). Official advice to evacuate was issued to affected towns. No death or injury was reported, but this typhoon was a reminder of the threats of landslides caused by heavy and intensive rain. In addition, road closures caused four neighbourhoods to be isolated (Kagawa University, 2004). A big debris flow occupied the playground of a primary school, where an evacuation centre was located.

River floods and debris flow: the 23rd typhoon (2004)

The 23rd typhoon crossed Shikoku Island on the 20 October. The local meteorological observatory issued a warning of heavy rains and flooding at 9:49. The east side of Kagawa prefecture experienced a record-breaking total accumulated rainfall of 674mm during the event. In Takamatsu city, the total rainfall was 285mm. This rainfall caused the Kasuga river to be flooded, and it broke dykes along the river (Kagawa University, 2004). In contrast to the 16th typhoon, which mainly affected the port and Central Business District (CBD) area, floods caused by the 23rd typhoon were observed in various places in Takamatsu city. The rain from this typhoon caused a number of landslides and debris flows in the east side of Kagawa prefecture. They impacted houses and agricultural lands (Nishino et al., 2005).

The casualties, injuries, inundation and damages to facilities caused by the three typhoons recorded in Kagawa prefecture are summarised in Table 4.1.

Perception of residents: 2004 typhoons

The author conducted a questionnaire survey and qualitative interviews with residents on their perceptions and responses to the 2004 typhoons.

Questionnaire survey

A resident questionnaire survey was conducted in June 2018 to collect data on residents' experiences with natural hazards (including the 2004

Table 4.1 Summary of three typhoons that affected Kagawa prefecture

	16th typhoon	*21st typhoon*	*23rd typhoon*
Death	3	0	11
Injury	6	0	28
House collapse (whole)	1	1	48
House damage (partial)	245	42	388
House inundation (above floor level)	5,872	46	4,431
House inundation (below floor level)	16,088	240	13,336
Damages to public facilities	98	183	2,364
Impact on agriculture	8,568 ha	1,800 ha	ha not available

(Source: author's compilation of the data in Kagawa University, 2004)

typhoons) and how they are preparing for future hazards.[4] The questionnaire survey was conducted on both an online platform (survey monkey) and using a paper-based form. Participants were recruited through local newspapers and the newsletter of the local university. In addition, a paper-based questionnaire sheet was distributed at a public symposium held at the local university. Residents who participated in the symposium were asked to fill in the questionnaire survey during the symposium. Two hundred sixty-four residents participated in the online questionnaire survey, and 51 residents participated in the paper-based questionnaire survey, equalling 315 responses in total. After scrutiny, 313 responses were deemed as valid.

When measured against population data obtained from the Basic Resident Register (as of 1 February 2018), our sample skews slightly disproportionately male. In terms of proportion by age group, we have a higher proportion of respondents between 20 and 59 years old and a lower proportion of those above 60 years old. More than half of the participants had lived in Takamatsu for over 15 years, implying that they were present during the 2004 typhoon hazards. The majority of participants who had lived in the city for over 15 years remembered the 16th typhoon of 2004. Amongst those (n=153) respondents, 43.8 % were at home, 11.8 % were at their workplace, 1.3 % were at their family's place, 1.3 % were at evacuation centres and the rest were either elsewhere or they left the answer blank. Among the respondents to the questionnaire survey, 35 participants lived in the flooded area at the time of the storm surge. Two people responded that they evacuated. One person stated that they started evacuation after the flooding started and another responded that they made the decision to evacuate before the warning was issued. Those who did not evacuate thought 'my home is safe.' This is a find-ing from a small number of responses but is consistent with the findings of Oikawa and Mukaitani (2005), who collected a larger number of responses (about 1,400). They also found that many people were informed that flood-ing might occur, but residents did not accept that this could really happen to 'them' and did not take action (such as moving cars to higher grounds or evacuating) until very late.[5] Answers to the question 'Will you evacuate at the time of the next typhoon event?' were mixed. Some answered 'yes' with reasons of: 'life is most important,' 'I know my neighbourhood is risky according to the hazard map' and 'my house was flooded before.' Partici-pants who answered 'no' stated: 'my house is safe,' 'I am not sure if it would be safe to evacuate.' Participants who answered 'not sure' stated: 'it will depend on the situation,' 'I am not sure where the safe place is.'

Amongst all participants of the questionnaire survey, 8 (2.5%) stated that they attend all evacuation drills and 25 participants (7.9%) stated that they attend when they can. The rest of the respondents answered that they do not attend because 'I am too busy to attend' or 'I do not think the drill is use-ful.' In the free comment space, they wrote 'I think people here have low awareness of the risks of natural hazards,' 'I am concerned about the Nankai Trough earthquake,' 'We need more useful evacuation drills' and 'We need to have more detailed disaster mitigation measures.'

Narratives

The author conducted interviews with residents in March and June 2017 and organised community workshops in June-July 2019. Fifteen residents from a range of neighbourhoods affected by the 2004 typhoons participated in the interviews. In terms of community workshops, five communities that were most affected by the storm surge were selected and their neighbour-hood association leaders were contacted by the author with the support of the city council (see Appendix).

At interviews and workshops, residents shared their experiences and per-ceptions of the 2004 typhoons. The following are narratives of residents extracted from interview/workshop transcripts, on the topics of storm surge, heavy rain/flood, evacuation and community responses.

Storm surge:

> '*It was only in 2004 when this neighbourhood was flooded for the first time. Our neighbourhood is located on higher ground than the sur-rounding neighbourhoods. We never expected the flood to happen. The water level rose very quietly. We did not know that water had already come from the harbour. The electricity blacked out and I realised when*

I went down to the shop. Nobody was ready because we thought that the typhoon had passed.' (P1, shop owner, CBD).

'As a fisherman, I understand risks by reading the wind. At the time of the storm surge, we did not move our boats/ships from our usual harbour because this is historically a very protected harbour due to its topography. The harbour itself is well protected against typhoons. Therefore our colleagues from other towns bring their boats here. Our town was flooded to waist level but we did not need to evacuate while we were at this harbour.' (P 2 and 3, fishermen, town facing the Seto Inland Sea).

'At the time of the storm surge, my house was flooded. The evacuation order was issued but because water was flowing, I decided to stay home and I went upstairs. My area is on low ground. The river nearby is very narrow. After the storm surge, the river was widened under the measures decided by the Law Concerning Special Fiscal Aid for Coping with Disasters.[6]*'* (P4 and 5, retired, volunteer)

'We realised there was a storm surge because of the beeping of cars. Three of our cars got flooded. There was no evacuation order. I never knew that the storm surge was such a disaster. It was not raining so much.' (P11 and P12)

'The water rose very quietly and there was no evacuation order. As a fire brigade, we got a call and were asked to help an older lady to evacuate to the school. It was around 10pm and the river started to flood. At around midnight the neighbourhood was all flooded.' (participant to a workshop at Kita neighbourhood association)

Heavy rain/floods:

'(At the time of typhoon 23rd), I was told to evacuate and I went to the evacuation centre (school) with my 3 dogs. But there was no one there. The teachers at the school were asking us to let them know if we needed anything (they had never organised an evacuation centre before so they were nervous). My house was flooded and shoe boxes were floating. The water came from the river behind my house. The river is usually dry at that time. They said that a hazard like this happens once every 50 years. The water receded relatively quickly and I started to clean the next day.' (P6, retired)

'(At the time of typhoon 23rd), The rain was extraordinary. I heard rumbling noises twice. A landslide happened behind the house and the mud came into our shed. I went upstairs because water was coming to our house. I was very scared. I changed into swimwear and also even prepared a swim ring. I thought I might die. It was so loud because of the rain. Our house, which is 3m above sea level,

survived. I suspect that my father-in-law had raised the house level. The harbour nearby was also flooded.' (P7, retired)

'Many things including pieces of timber flowed into the house. I never expected this. Because my house is very old, the water flowed into house a lot although the base of the house did not move. The cleaning was a tough thing. The water marks and dust never go away.' (P14)

'I needed to wait for a while until the water receded. It was too dangerous to drive home. I detoured to a mountain route to get home.' (P15)

Evacuation:

'We have yet to have evacuation plans.' (P 2 and 3, fishermen)

'I was driving but because the water level was rising, I got out of the car and hung on the electricity pole and waited for help. There was no one but a man who owned a boat came and helped me. He offered to let me stay at his place (upstairs, because the downstairs was flooded).' (P13, part-time, working in CBD)

'In terms of the storm surge, we really do not have a way to evacuate because of the location of this town, which is in-between two rivers. The only way is to go upstairs (vertical evacuation) or go south.' (participant to a workshop at Kita neighbourhood association)

'When I realised, the road in front of my house was already like a river so I couldn't evacuate. Many older people stayed home and were upstairs or on a table if they did not go upstairs.' (participant to a workshop at Matsushima neighbourhood association).

Community responses:

'I shared food with my neighbours.' (P6)

'We have a Neighbourhood Association but I had heard nothing.' (P6)

'I am not able to walk fast and I hesitate to ask for help from a city public servant. I am not sure what I could do.' (P7)

'My father-in-law was talking about what we really need to do is upgrade the dyke on the Kasuga river. The guidelines from my Neighbourhood Association are quite scanty. There was no help or training.'(P14)

'The storm surge was a wake-up call and we started to respond earlier at the time of the next typhoon.' (participant to a workshop at Kita neighbourhood association)

Challenges faced with increasing risks of natural hazard

The data collected through the questionnaire survey, interviews and community workshops indicate that there are various challenges in coping with disaster risks in Takamatsu. These are summarised into four themes: awareness, leadership, community ties and new challenges. Each theme is discussed in this section with suggestions to address.

Awareness

The biggest concern that was shared was the unchanged level of awareness of disaster risks in Takamatsu. This is partly because there have been fewer critical events (compared with other parts of Japan).

> '*We have been lucky. Because of the Shikoku mountains, we didn't have many disasters compared with other neighbouring prefectures.*' (P9 and P10)
>
> '*I really think that the awareness of people in Takamatsu is very low.*' (P8, P14)

In some communities, the awareness has been enhanced since 2004. However, it varies.

> '*The 2004 typhoons definitely changed our attitudes.*' (P14)
>
> '*We had very low awareness but the 2004 event changed our mind. After the 2011 tsunami in north Japan, I think it really started to change. Now we have 1,400 participants in an evacuation drill every year. It is important that we do this every year, otherwise it is easy to forget the risks of disasters.*' (participant in a workshop at Kita neighbourhood association)
>
> '*Older people know that we have risks of floods in this area and how we have enhanced preparedness so far. However younger people (under 50 years old) don't know much about it, therefore they have low awareness. We also have liquefaction risks here but nobody have experienced this.*' (participant in a workshop at Kasuga town neighbourhood association)

Residents tend to forget about the risks if they are not exposed to the hazard or reminded regularly of potential disasters. Also, they tend to think that their house is safe. This is called normalcy bias in disaster psychology (Katada, 2020). Evacuation training is a useful means for them to re-educate and check how they may plan to protect their lives, as well as receive updates. The challenge is how to encourage residents to recognise the importance of regular training and participate. In the community, which has a low number of participants attending training, the awareness of risks is likely to be low. In such a community, residents do not prioritise preparing for disasters. It is important that authorities use every opportunity to disseminate the risk information to the residents. Oral tradition (Nakanishi & Black, 2018) is an effective way to pass on the narratives to the next generations, but this is not enough. A strategic approach to risk education, and incentives to participate, are necessary.

Leadership

Raising awareness is associated with leadership. Both prefecture and city governments have offices of disaster risk management. At the time of an emergency, they work with local fire brigades and neighbourhood association leaders. Their collaboration is expected to be effective and efficient. However, officers of these bodies do not necessarily have extensive experience on managing disasters.

> '*There is also a gap in understanding between the prefecture, the city and local fire brigades like us.*' (participant in a workshop at Kasuga town neighbourhood association)

At a local/neighbourhood level, leaders of neighbourhood associations play a critical role. However, their awareness and efforts vary.

> '*The leader of our neighbourhood association changes every year and it is hard for them to keep the motivation to address the challenges. I think the awareness level varies by individual and the gap is significant.*' (P7)
>
> '*Our current neighbourhood association leader is very keen to raise awareness and train residents. We have regular evacuation drills and we also borrow storage in a school, where we store emergency goods. We also have evacuation goods at home.*' (P9 and P10)
>
> '*I am currently the leader of the neighbourhood association and we are really working hard on evacuation training. There are two drills: one is assuming an earthquake and another one is assuming a tsunami and 4–500 people participate every year. We have done this 8 times already. We also have prepared in case residents need to stay in evacuation centres for some days. We discuss how to help each other.*' (P11 and P12)

Residents living in neighbourhoods where they don't see a strong leadership commented:

> '*I have not heard anything from the neighbourhood association (about drill etc.).*' (P6)
> '*I think the challenge is leadership. Having said this, I understand that it is important to protect my life myself.*' (P14)

Along with raising awareness, making leadership consistent across all neighbourhood associations, fire brigades and the relevant offices of city and prefecture governments would be beneficial in enhancing preparedness. This may be addressed by seminars and training by experts from the local university, where there is a disaster and crisis management program.

Community ties

The leaders of neighbourhood associations all raised the concern that assisting people in need of help at the time of evacuation is a big challenge. One big factor is residents' unwillingness to be part of neighbourhood associations because they do not want to take part in organised events and other activities and do not wish to take responsibility for their neighbourhoods or are too busy to do so. After the revision of the Disaster Counter Measure Fundamental Law in 2013, it became mandatory that local councils maintain an updated list of people who need assistance for evacuation. In Takamatsu, the city council administers this list. Despite this law, many local neighbourhood associations struggle to provide this list.

> '*We are doing evacuation drills every year under different themes. We have hazards maps of floods and landslides. What we are working hard on at the moment is to help people who need assistance at the time of evacuation. We are making a list of who will help whom but it's very difficult because not many people belong to neighbourhood associations now. We need strong incentives to be part of the association otherwise they (people who don't belong in neighbourhood associations) will not get useful information at the time of crisis.*' (leader, Ritsurin town neighbourhood association)
> '*There are many people who don't belong to neighbourhood associations but we need to help them in the crisis no matter if they belong or not. It would help us a lot if we have more information about people living here.*' (leader, Matsushima town neighbourhood association)

> '*Because the majority of residents have been living here for a long time, we are quite tight-knit. This may be a bit unusual. The challenge is how to involve younger people and also how to help older people who need assistance.*' (P11 and P12)

In one neighbourhood, they were seeking for a way to use the information technology (IT) system to understand the cohort of residents.

> '*We have apartments. We don't know who is living here because the residents in apartments highly prioritise their privacy. However we have an ICT system being used in our medical centre and the data might be used for managing evacuations in the future. The medical centre could be a disaster management hub for the neighbourhood.*' (Marugamemachi town neighbourhood association)

Forging community ties is a difficult challenge to address. Japanese society is becoming diverse, and many people are not interested in being a member of neighbourhood associations. The old-style community, based on agricultural village society (see Chapter 3), in which residents helped each other to protect themselves from natural hazards and the associated loss of community assets, no longer exist. As the neighbourhood association system has become less effective, no alternative system has emerged (Hiroi, 2019). As it is unrealistic to recover the 'help each other system' in the community, the use of technology (as per the narrative above) will be essential in the obtaining of information and providing necessary support to people in need. Community ties may not be created in this way, but there is a need for a system by which residents help each other in an emergency.

New challenges

For the communities of Takamatsu, a storm surge is still a main concern because they have typhoons every year. However, the unknown risk of a tsunami is an even bigger fear for authorities, fire brigades and community leaders, because residents have experienced a storm surge already and have improved some infrastructure. Authorities are more concerned about how to cope with the risks of a tsunami associated with the Nankai Trough earthquake in the near future. Some residents understand the risks of a tsunami, but many don't take it seriously. The level of understanding of the risks is inconsistent throughout the city.

> '*After the storm surge the prefecture government published the hazard map because they are concerned about the Nankai Trough earthquake and tsunami.*' (P1, shop owner, CBD)

'*The tsunami will come to our area from every direction. I cannot imagine how the water will come to our town.*' (Matsushima town neighbourhood association)

'*We have very low awareness of the tsunami.*' (Marugamemachi town neighbourhood association)

Although information on tsunami risk is disseminated from the city government, not all residents are aware of it. In addition, most residents have never experienced a tsunami before, which means that there is no reference to follow. It is critical to share the information, ensure a certain level of awareness across the community and devise evacuation strategy that is well disseminated. Evacuation training in the case of a tsunami is also important to enhance preparedness. In summary, the challenge is to raise awareness of typhoons, storm surges and tsunamis and develop a comprehensive strategy to manage risks. Local governments (prefecture, city), fire brigades, neighbourhood associations and residents all have roles in reducing risks to the whole community. It is important that they maintain a state-of-the-art knowledge of risks and train residents how to respond at a time of crisis. In this way, community ties can be strengthened through nurturing the culture of 'helping' and 'sharing' that once existed in many Japanese communities. This will be critical for this ageing and depopulating mid-sized city in Japan.

Appendix

Table 4.2 List of interview participants

ID	Address (Town)	Age group*	Gender
P1	Marugame machi	60s	Male
P2	Aji cho	50s	Male
P3	Aji cho	60s	Male
P4	Kasuga cho	70s	Male
P5	Kita cho	70s	Female
P6	Tamura cho	70s	Female
P7	Hiketa cho	60s	Female
P8	Ban cho	90s	Female
P9	Matsunawa cho	70s	Female
P10	Matsunawa cho	70s	Male
P11	Fukuoka cho	60s	Male
P12	Fukuoka cho	60s	Female
P13	Yura cho	60s	Female
P14	Kawashima cho	60s	Female
P15	Kagawa cho	60s	Female

*As of the time of interview.

Table 4.3 List of community workshops

Neighbourhood association	Number of participants
Ritsurin town	4
Kita town	12
Kasuga town	13
Matushima town	9
Marugamemachi town	2

Notes

1 According to the Japan Meteorological Agency website: www.data.jma.go.jp/fcd/yoho/typhoon/position_table/table2004.html Accessed on 5 April 2022. *Written in Japanese.*
2 Nankai Trough extends from Suruga Warf (Shizuoka) to Hyuganada (Miyazaki) between the Eurasian and Philippine Sea plates. The Nankai Trough earthquake occurs approximately every 100 to 150 years. Over 75 years have passed since the last quake in 1944; the next one is expected in the near future.
3 As of November 2021, this record has not been broken.
4 This timing was important – in Kagawa, no major hazard had occurred since 2004 until the date of the survey (the floods described in Chapter 6 occurred after the survey was conducted). The survey successfully captured the perceptions and preparedness of residents in a nonemergency situation.
5 The official number of evacuated residents is not available.
6 Implemented in 1961.

References

Hiroi, Y. (2019). *Design of depopulating society (Jinko gensho shakai no dezain).* Tokyo, Japan: Toyo Keizai Inc (the translation of the title is made by the author) [Written in Japanese].

Kagawa University. (2004). *Report of typhoon disaster investigation task force.* Takamatsu, Japan: Kagawa University (the translation of the title is made by the author) [Written in Japanese].

Katada, T. (2020). *Hitoni yorisou bousai.* Tokyo, Japan: Shueisha Inc [Written in Japanese].

Kihara, H., Niwa, Y., Tanaka, K., & Wada, H. (2012). *History of Kagawa prefecture second edition.* Tokyo, Japan: Yamakawa Shuppansha (the translation of the title is made by the author).

Nakanishi, H., & Black, J. (2018). Implicit and explicit knowledge in flood evacuations with a case study of Takamatsu, Japan. *International Journal of Disaster Risk Reduction, 28,* 788–797. https://doi.org/10.1016/j.ijdrr.2018.02.008

Nishino, K., Hasegawa, S., Yamanaka, M., Masuda, T., & Moriya, H. (2005). The situation of landslide and debris flow caused by the typhoon 23rd, 2004. *Jiban-saigai Jiban kankyo mondai ronbun shu (Journal of Foundation Disaster and*

Foundation Disaster Issues), 5(29) (the translation of the title is made by the author) [Written in Japanese].

Oikawa, Y., & Mukaitani, M. (2005). Characteristics of human behavior in high tide disaster by typhoon 0416 and 0418. *Japan Society of Civil Engineers.* http://library.jsce.or.jp/jsce/open/00039/200506_no31/pdf/179.pdf (Accessed on 9 April 2022) [Written in Japanese].

5 Community as a hub of response

Kumamoto earthquake of 2016

The shake

The Kumamoto region is located in the middle of Kyushu Island. The climate is relatively warm. The region is blessed with the Ariake Sea in the west and Mt. Aso in the east. The capital city of Kumamoto prefecture, Kumamoto city, has a population of more than 700,000 (the total population of Kumamoto prefecture is 1.7 million (as of October 2021[1]). The population is concentrated in the urban area.

On the night of 14 April 2016, a magnitude 6.5 earthquake struck the Kumamoto region on the Japanese island of Kyushu (Figure 5.1). Two days later, another shock (magnitude of 7.3) struck the same area. Later, the second shock was determined as the 'main' shock by the Bureau of Meteorology.[2] There were 273 casualties and 2,809 injuries according to the Cabinet Office.[3] As many as 163,500 houses were completely or partially destroyed or damaged. At its peak, a total of 185,125 people sought shelter in 1,166 evacuation centres[4] (Cabinet Office, 2019). Also, 190 landslides were recorded. The Kyushu area, although it has typhoons and heavy rain every year, is relatively less prepared for earthquakes compared to other areas in Japan (e.g., *Tohoku*, where there have been mega earthquakes historically, including the 2011 disaster). Due to the fact that it is located in the main path of typhoons and active volcanoes, the focus of disaster management had been on these two major hazards in Kyushu. This 2016 earthquake was a wake-up call for people and authorities in Kyushu, reminding them that they should also prepare for earthquakes and tsunamis, given that the southern part of the island faces the Pacific Ocean. Despite the severity of the 2011 earthquake and tsunami that had occurred in the northern side of the country, the unprepared local governments and communities in Kyushu struggled to manage the immediate response and the process of recovery. In this chapter, the recovery process is outlined along with the disaster recovery lifecycle (Nakanishi et al., 2014; Blackman et al., 2017) to review the issues and the knowledge gained through the process. This is followed by

DOI: 10.4324/9781003150190-5

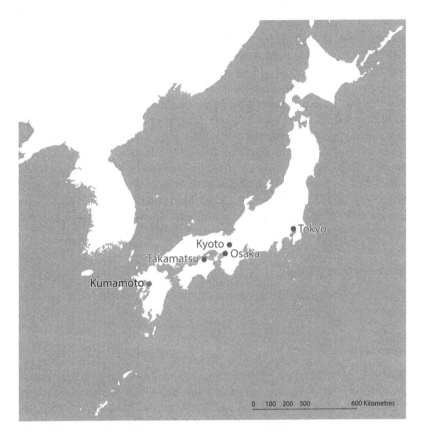

Figure 5.1 Location of Kumamoto region

an analysis of the collaborative actions of government, community and local universities, which helped the management of recovery. Although surrounding prefectures were also affected, this chapter focuses on Kumamoto prefecture, which was most affected.

On the day after the first quake, the local newspaper reported that about 44,000 people were evacuating in 505 shelters in Kumamoto. It also reported on the damage to utility services, public transport, air transport, roads and communications etc. (Kumamoto Nichinichi Newspaper, 2016a). The summary of interruptions is as follows:

PUBLIC TRANSPORT: Kyushu Shinkansen and main railway lines (JR and private), bus services were ceased.
AIR TRANSPORT: flights between Kumamoto and Tokyo was cancelled.
LAND TRANSPORT: Kyushu expressway was partly closed.

COMMUNICATION: the mobile network was not available in parts of Mashiki town and Kosa town.

ELECTRICITY: at its peak, about 477,000 households lost access.

GAS: at its peak, over 105,000 households had no access.

WATER: at its peak, about 445,900 households had no access.

The second shake on 16 April further impacted the region. The death toll increased and JR lines were stopped. Electricity outages and disruptions to water supply continued. Many buildings were damaged. The turrets and stone walls of Kumamoto Castle[5] collapsed (Kumamoto Nichinichi Newspaper, 2016b). As of 31 March 2017, the number of aftershocks counted was 4,284. In total, 3,406 facilities/infrastructure were damaged (Kumamoto City, 2017). In total, 4,303 temporary houses were provided in 16 jurisdictions. In addition to this, 27,813 public/private housing units were secured for people in need (Cabinet Office, 2019).

Immediate responses

The first responses of each government[6] and volunteer organisation are outlined in the following sections:

National government

On 14 April, at 21:31, the Prime Minister's office set up a counter measures office. The headquarters for major disaster countermeasures (HMDC) was announced at 22:10 (closed on 30 November 2018). On 15 April, an investigative team left for Kumamoto at 6:40. At 10:40, a local headquarters for the national government for major disaster countermeasures was set up (closed on 16 September 2016). At 13:00, the first meeting of the national government's headquarters team and Kumamoto prefecture's headquarter team was held. At 17:00, a second meeting of the national government's headquarters team and Kumamoto prefecture's headquarters team was held. On 16 April, the Prime Minister's office announced the implementation of 'push' style[7] support to the affected area.

Local governments

Kumamoto Prefecture:

The prefecture's regional disaster risk plan regulates that the headquarters for major disaster countermeasures (HMDC) are to be established when an earthquake of *Shindo* 6[8] and above happens. At 10:40pm on 14 April, the governor of Kumamoto ordered the Self-Defence Forces to launch a disaster relief operation. At 0:30 on the 15 April, the first meeting of the prefecture's HMDC was held. The prefecture's HMDC corresponded with the national government's HMDC and other national department offices to arrange necessary measures.

Kumamoto city:

> Kumamoto city has also legislated to set up a HMDC in the event of a large-scale natural hazard. After the first quake, a HMDC was arranged at the city council. At 1am on 15 April, the first meeting of the city's HMDC was held. Information was given about casualties and damages to infrastructure and facilities. The mayor requested blankets and water to be provided to affected residents and called for information on what was needed. He also requested measures to prevent economy class syndrome[9] in those who stayed in their cars.

Volunteer organisations

After the Kobe (Great Hanshin) earthquake, many local and national networks of non-profit organisations (NPO) for disaster relief were established (Suzuki et al., 2003).

Japan National Council of Social Welfare:

> During 14–16 April, staff members were sent to the affected areas to investigate the needs of volunteers. NPOs were called upon to provide staff to help with the delivery and distribution of emergency goods.

The Kumamoto prefecture and city council of social welfare arranged a volunteer group to help clean up affected houses and relocate residents to temporary housing.

Japan Voluntary Organizations Active in Disaster (JVOAD) Network:

> As of 31 August, around 300 organisations had participated in volunteer activities. The following is the summary of the main activities. Many organisations joined the network of organisations called "Hinokuni[10] Kaigi" (HK).

18th of April: representatives of 21 organisations including the Cabinet Office and the Ministry of Health, Labour and Welfare held a meeting to discuss support for the shelters.

27th of April: HK member organisations and prefectures started to distribute relief supplies to shelters.

5th of May: NPOs, national government and the prefecture's Council of Social Welfare discussed the operation of shelters.

10th of May: HK member organisations and city council started fortnightly meetings to discuss and share the situation and challenges.

12th of May: HK member organisations and authorities of Mashiki town[11] decided to organise a fortnightly meeting.

15th of May: Mashiki town officially requested JVOAD to provide help until the end of August.

Volunteer organisations and their networks played a significant role in assisting relief activities. They inspected the shelters, shared information on the activities of each organisation and ensured that their activities complemented each other (Cabinet Office, 2019).

The road to recovery

Recovery from major natural hazards is a long-term process and it is illustrated by the disaster recovery lifecycle (Nakanishi et al., 2014). In the case of the Kumamoto earthquake, the prefecture stated that the restoration stage would commence one month after the event. Figure 5.2 shows the disaster recovery lifecycle of the Kumamoto earthquake (as of July 2021). The prefecture announced priorities for recovery in 2017. They were 1) rebuilding of houses, 2) disposal of disaster debris, 3) restoration of access to Mt. Aso (road and railway), 4) restoration of Kumamoto Castle, 5) recovery of Mashiki town, 6) recovery of affected businesses, 7) recovery of affected agriculture businesses, 8) implementation of an airport upgrade, 9) development of the cruise hub of Yatsushiro port and 10) successfully organising international sports events in 2018 and 2019 (Kumamoto Prefecture, 2017). The prefecture published a report on their progress towards the targets in November 2019. With the exception of South Aso Railway (expected to start operation in 2023) and the new terminal building of Kumamoto airport (expected to open in 2023), the projects associated with these priorities were expected to be completed by 2020. Therefore, in this chapter, it is assumed that the restoration stage ended in 2020 and the long-term recovery phase started soon afterwards.

This section focuses on the ongoing recovery process of Mashiki town, which was devastated by the earthquake.

Figure 5.2 Disaster recovery lifecycle: case of Kumamoto earthquake

Machiki town is located almost in the middle of Kumamoto prefecture, which is 8.5km from the prefectural government office and 7.5km from Kumamoto airport. The area is 6,568 hectares. The population was around 33,000 as of 2014 (Mashiki Town, 2018). In addition to agricultural lands and rice fields, the town has modern urban residential areas.

The town published the renewed disaster prevention plan on 30 June 2020. Furthermore, on 30 April 2021, Mashiki town renewed its 'disaster prevention basics regulations' and declared it to be a 'safe town.' The following is the trajectory of the town's activities gleaned from its town brochures.

14–17 July 2016: A meeting of ward leaders, the town mayor, the staff of the town's disaster prevention section and experts from local universities was held to discuss the recovery plan. A schedule of public meetings between 28 July and 20 August was agreed upon.

5 August: The first recovery plan committee meeting was held (there were 23 participants) to review the impact from the earthquake as well as the disaster recovery basic policies and the feedback from residents.

The main points discussed were:

- It is important to review the responses of the town council.
- Listen to younger people's suggestions.
- Discuss the allocation of town offices at the special interest group meeting.
- Discuss the need for a planned rebuild of the town.
- Collaboration with residents is critical. This needs to be considered along with the redevelopment of communities.
- There needs to be support for affected businesses.
- There is a need for a symbol of recovery.
- This town is the hub of recovery for Kyushu.
- We need to work carefully so that we acknowledge the opinions of residents.
- There needs to be an innovative and flexible plan regardless of past experience.

The committee agreed to create special interest groups (SIGs) on 1) living/life, 2) town planning and 3) industry/business matters. These SIGs would develop a draft of the recovery plan by early October.

The town estimated that the budget for recovery was 700 million yen (USD 640 million).

10 November: The third recovery plan committee meeting was held, followed by the completion of the draft recovery plan on 11 November. The draft recovery plan was published and open for comments (by 28 November).

8 December: The fourth recovery plan committee meeting was held to discuss updating the draft recovery plan to reflect residents' comments and a schedule for recovery.

20 December: The recovery plan was approved at the town council assembly. The interim report on 'the state of safety measures towards the recovery of town centres' was released by the Ministry of Land, Infrastructure and Transport.

12 January 2017: The schedule of public meetings on the designated recovery promotion areas was released on the town brochure. The information sessions on the recovery plan were also scheduled and a symposium was held in February.

10 March 2017: A decision was made to go ahead with the designated areas. Under this decision, any plan that changed the topography, required new building development or required repairing or extending buildings needed the approval of the town mayor (during 10 March 2017 until 13 April 2018).

1 April 2017: An announcement of the support project for the repair and reinforcement of affected houses was published in a town brochure.

28 April 2017: A support scheme for repairing affected agricultural lands was announced in a town brochure.

8–18 June 2017: Information sessions on public housing (for residents whose houses were affected) were held. About 800 residents participated. It was expected that the construction would start in June 2018 (for detached, 1-storey houses) and November 2018 for apartments.

27 July 2017: The first committee meeting on public housing was held. Eighteen members (including experts, leader of wards and town assembly members) participated.

The second questionnaire survey on living conditions was distributed to residents in summer 2017.

11 August 2017: The first committee meeting on 'the preservation of the memory and experiences of the Kumamoto earthquake' was held. Eighteen members (including experts, leader of wards and town assembly members) participated. Special interest groups on 'education/training of disaster prevention,' 'reservation and utilisation of disaster remnants and memory' and 'memorial park of the disaster' were arranged.

28 August: The second committee meeting on public housing was held.

27 September: The third committee meeting on public housing was held and it was decided that 680 households that meet the eligibility would be allocated to public housing. This was the standard number used for development, and this number would be re-evaluated after consideration of the progress of residents' independent repair/reconstruction. This suggestion was sent to the town for review and approval.

9, 11, 12 November: Info sessions on the 'town centre land readjustment project' were held.

1 December 2017: The town announced that it had exchanged partnership agreements with three universities in Kumamoto (Kumamoto University, Prefectural University of Kumamoto and Kumamoto Gakuen University) in a town brochure on 1 December.

20 December 2017: The 'town centre land readjustment project' was rejected by the city/town planning council.

15 January–28 February 2018: Applications for public housing started.

16 January 2018: The first committee meeting on 'desired repairment and use of public facilities' was held. Ten people including experts, assembly members and leaders of each ward participated. The committee discussed the future of three community facilities in the town.

5 March 2018: The 'town centre land readjustment project' was approved by the city/town planning council, subject to 'considering opinions/requests of residents and reducing their concerns.'

14 May 2018: The town accepted 'the Mashiki town recovery plan (evacuation routes and direction)' at the fourth recovery plan committee meeting.

20 and 22 July 2018: Information sessions on the 'town centre land readjustment project' were held.

August 2018: 'A basic concept on new residential areas' was released.

31 July and 13 August: 'Mashiki comprehensive planning committee' meetings were held. These were to discuss moving towards the development of the sixth comprehensive planning strategy.

18, 19, 25 and 26 August: A lottery was held to determine the allocation of public housing.

October 2018: The use of temporary housing was extended for another year.

22 October–11 November 2018: Residents' opinions (public comments) on the sixth comprehensive planning strategy were called for.

26 October 2018: Four road upgrade projects were approved. An information session for residents was held in December.

During November 2018: An introductory session for residents moving into the same public housing complex was held. Residents had the opportunity to meet their new neighbours over morning/afternoon tea.

19 November: The sixth (final) Mashiki comprehensive planning committee meeting was held. At the meeting, the members discussed the revised draft strategy and checked that it reflected the comments from residents.

13–14 February 2019: Info sessions on the widening of Kiyama Miyazono road were held.

12 and 14 February 2019: Info sessions on the changes to the bus route were held.

15 February and 16 March 2019: A residents' workshop on the design of the new town council building was held.

15 March 2019: Reallocation of temporary housing due to low % of usage (because many residents left for new homes) was announced in the town brochure.

June–July 2019: An introduction session for residents moving into the same public housing complex was held. Residents had opportunities to meet new neighbours over morning/afternoon tea.

October 2019: An information session on the Miyazono Ichinosako area redevelopment was held.

1 October 2019: Further reallocation of temporary housing due to low % of usage (because many residents left for new homes) was announced in the town brochure.

24 and 25 December 2019: Keys for public housing were provided to residents of 40 units. The remaining 595 units were to be completed and keys provided by the end of March (announced in the town brochure on 27 December 2019).

The draft plan of the new town hall's basic design was completed and comments from residents were received (announced in the town brochure on 17 February 2020). The new town hall's development is ongoing as of March 2022 (34.2% of the construction work completed).

17 February 2020: The draft revision of the town master plan was made and comments from residents were called for in the town brochure. The info session was held on 29 February.

16 March 2020: A change of bus route to improve its level of service was announced in the town brochure.

15 July 2020: A change of bus route to improve its level of service was announced in the town brochure.[12]

Collaboration with the local university

In the process of recovery, local universities have played a key role in supporting the process and communicating with residents about their aspirations and requests for local governments.

The Kumamoto University (the local national university) established a 'Kumamoto recovery support project' (*Kumamoto Fukko Shien Project*) on 14 June 2016 and arranged seven project teams, listed as follows[13] (Kumamoto University, 2016).

1   Disaster recovery design project
2   Mt. Aso region natural hazard mitigation project
3   Kumamoto hydrologic circulation system protection project

4 Restoration support of cultural assets damaged by the earthquake
5 Recovery of industry project
6 Support for health care/medical sector
7 Support for volunteer activities for recovery

In this book, the author focuses on the activities of the project team's disaster recovery design project. The following are the activities of the project team as extracted from its newsletters.[14]

June–July 2016: Students of Kumamoto University Conducted interviews with residents of 58 households residing in temporary housing to understand their perceptions about and prospects for future living. The interviews continued after August. As of 3 September, a total of 675 households had participated in the interviews.

19 October 2016: The Mashiki Lab (a facility built by the university) opened. This facility was developed to promote conversations between residents, university staff and students on town planning. University staff and students were present every Saturday from 2–5pm and encouraged residents to pop in and talk. Events were also held here.

During 2017: the university staff and students continued to engage with residents through weekly visits to Mashiki Lab and the organisation of a number of events.

February 2017: Students' ideas on recovery were exhibited at the lab. The findings of the residents' interviews (1,200 household participated in the end) were shared and discussed.

26 October 2017: The first anniversary event was held, with a guest lecture on the recovery from the Kobe (Great Hanshin) earthquake and a photo exhibition of Mashiki's recovery.

21 February 2018: The Mashiki Lab staff and students organised an event titled 'Open Lab to discuss the new prefecture road at the temporary town hall building.'

March 2018: Design ideas were developed for each school jurisdiction by students. These were presented at the lab.

28 May 2018: The second residents' forum was held to discuss the new prefecture road by the lab staff and students.

10 July 2018: A symposium titled 'Designing Recovery' was held by inviting a guest lecturer.

The model of the new prefecture road was displayed at the Lab.

19 October 2019: An event to discuss present and future progress was held. Students had been continuing to study the spatial design of the town.

November–December 2019: A questionnaire survey on disaster prevention was distributed to all households (response rate: 32%).

22 February 2020: Students' activities and study outcomes were reported at the lab. Models of the design of open space were displayed at the lab.

Due to the COVID-19 outbreak, the lab was closed for most of 2020. It reopened in November 2020. However, the lab has been closed from time to time due to the continuing outbreaks during 2021.[15]

Lessons and challenges

The author had an opportunity to discuss the trajectory of recovery, lessons and challenges with experts who are teaching and researching at Kumamoto University. These experts[16] are core members of the Mashiki Lab and the Team of Education and Research According Digital Archive (TERADA). The discussion focused on 'education on disaster risks and prevention,' 'successful cases of recovery based on collaboration' and 'challenges.'

Education on disaster risks and prevention

After the earthquake, the prefecture's board of education consulted the university regarding how it could enhance future opportunities for education on disaster risks and prevention. Meanwhile, there was a discussion on maintaining the three faults in Mashiki town, based on a request from a scholarly institution. The town council decided to declare the faults to be cultural assets (natural monuments) in June 2016. These assets were used at the children's summer school, which was held not long after the decision was made. This promoted discussion about how to utilise these assets for disaster education. This is also related to the 'succession of experience/lessons' that the university was aiming to contribute.

Successful cases of recovery based on collaboration

Hirata area: this area is located close to the centre of Mashiki town. The damage to roads was significant, and 30% of houses in this area had completely collapsed. A big fault ran behind this area (Sasaki et al., 2020). The residents and university students started a collaboration by walking around the town together to improve their knowledge of the town. Then, they started events in 2017 together. Along with events, they developed an evacuation strategy including a route plan (as part of the activity of the town planning committee). The leading body, the 'Hirata Yanagi Suigo planning committee' was established, and it has organised many events such as a town festival involving children.[17] Their aim is also to disseminate the lessons from the earthquake to the wider community for educational purposes. The activities in Hirata and collaboration with the university are continuing.

Fushijima area: This area is an agriculture village located on the terrace of the fault. About 35.5% of the houses were completely destroyed by the earthquake. Because this area is different from other areas of Mashiki town, it has had an independent committee for town planning since June 2017 (Sasaki et al., 2020). In this area, younger generations lead in town planning.[18] Just four months after establishing the committee, they submitted to the Mayor of Mashiki town their area plan, which was the result of twice monthly meetings and discussions. (Sasaki et al., 2020). After this, their focus shifted to volunteering to help people returning to normal life (e.g., cleaning up debris, organising events etc.). Collaboration with universities has helped these areas to move forward successfully.

'*They are utilising our Uni's Mashiki Lab very effectively.*' (Expert 2)

Meanwhile, the leaders of the two areas were organising their activities from a more long-term perspective.

'*They regard this project as a planning of their area, not just as a recovery.*' (Expert 1)

In these areas, the aforementioned 'succession of experience/lessons' is grounded in their activities.

'*They are connecting the "succession of experience/lessons" with the re-building of their life very well.*' (Expert 2)

Challenges

The big part of the discussion was on 'challenges' in long-term.

'*I understand this a long-term work. It is 5 years since the event now, and people are tired. We need to make a mechanism where we can work without much pressure. We will continue our activities for at least 5 years.*' (Expert 1)

'*My job is to contribute to make a place for a memorial service.*' (Expert 2)

'*It takes long time for affected people to accept their losses. I feel it may take even 20–30 years here.*' (Expert 3)

Education on disaster risks and prevention remained as a challenge – lessons of the earthquake was not utilised at the time of flood disaster in 2019.

'*Whilst the prefecture government is discussing their measures, Mashiki town has been discussing the town's original measures. A framework that the education is integrated to a routine work is needed.*' (Expert 3)

The prefecture's board of education created positions called 'chief of disaster prevention' in 2017, and allocated them to primary and junior high schools across the prefecture (Kumamoto Prefectural Board of Education, 2020). However, it is yet to be verified if this new system is working. At this stage, a teacher in a school takes this position in addition to their ordinary tasks. Their understanding of the role is not consistent.

'*The chief of disaster prevention is a person who establishes a network and uses it. They should be allocating tasks to others at the time of disaster. However some chiefs tend to do everything and take all the responsibilities.*' (Expert 3)

'*I am not sure if a teacher can do this. There should be a specialist located in each school.*' (Expert 1).

The recovery from the earthquake is not yet complete. The COVID-19 pandemic significantly affected activities such as residents' workshops, seminars and even just the normal casual interactions of residents, university staff and students. However, the residents are positive and are moving forward due to the 'cultural climate here.'[19] As of November 2021, after the COVID-19 state of emergency was lifted, many activities are being organised and residents have started to move forward.

Notes

1 According to Kumamoto prefecture's website.
2 The second shake being the main shock was the first time this happened in the historical record of earthquakes.
3 As of 12 April 2019.
4 This number is only those who stayed in dedicated shelters. There were many people who stayed in their cars, which revealed significant health risks.
5 Parts of Kumamoto Castle are designated as important national cultural assets.
6 Although surrounding prefectures were also affected, this chapter focuses on Kumamoto prefecture, which was most affected.
7 The 'push' style support has been included in the revised disaster countermeasure fundamental law (2012), based on the lessons from the North East Japan earthquake and tsunami (2011). Under the 'push' style support, goods that are regarded necessary are sent to the affected area, no matter whether the local governments of the affected area requested them or not.
8 *Shindo* is a unique seismic scale set out by the Japan Meteorological Agency, which is different from the magnitude. *Shindo* ranges from 0–7 and 7 is the maximum. The seismic intensity meter is placed around 600 points across Japan and recorded at these points. In the case of the Kumamoto earthquake, the first quake (14 April) was magnitude 6.5 and *Shindo* ranged from lower 5 to 7 and the second quake (16 April) was magnitude 7.3 and *Shindo* ranged from lower 5 to 7. At maximum *Shindo* 7, it is impossible to keep standing or move without crawling. People may be thrown through the air (www.jma.go.jp/jma/en/Activities/inttable.html; written in Japanese).

9 Also known as deep-vein thrombosis (DVT), this is caused by the formation of blood clots due to prolonged periods of physical inactivity (The Mainichi, 2016) https://mainichi.jp/english/articles/20160425/p2a/00m/0na/020000c Accessed on 8 April 2022.

10 Means 'Kumamoto prefecture.'

11 The most affected town by the Kumamoto earthquake.

12 This was the last town brochure published as of 9 April 2022.

13 The names of project teams are the author's translation, as there are no official English names.

14 Can be accessed here: https://cwmd.kumamoto-u.ac.jp/mashikilab/letter/ (written in Japanese).

15 The information of lab can be found on its Facebook page (www.facebook.com/profile.php?id=100044257257250; written in Japanese).

16 The areas of expertise are landscape design (expert 1), urban/town planning (expert 2) and disaster prevention and risk communication (expert 3).

17 Hirata Yanagi Suigo planning committee website (https://hiratayanagamizu.com/; written in Japanese).

18 Their activities are updated on their website (https://kumauq.com/; written in Japanese).

19 Based on the discussion with expert 1.

References

Blackman, D., Nakanishi, H., & Benson, A. M. (2017). Disaster resilience as a complex problem: Why linearity is not applicable for long-term recovery. *Technological Forecasting and Social Change, 121*, 89–98. https://doi.org/10.1016/j.techfore.2016.09.018

Cabinet Office. (2019). *Report of the impact of Kumamoto earthquake, 12 April 2019.* www.bousai.go.jp/updates/h280414jishin/pdf/h280414jishin_55.pdf (Accessed on 1 July 2021) [Written in Japanese].

Kumamoto City. (2017). *Record of 2016 Kumamoto earthquake (Kumamotoshi Shinsai Kirokushi).* www.city.kumamoto.jp/hpkiji/pub/detail.aspx?c_id=5&id=18725 (Accessed on 30 June 2021) [Written in Japanese].

Kumamoto Nichinichi Newspaper. (2016a, April 16). *Special edition.* Kumamoto, Japan: Kumamoto Nichinichi Newspaper [Written in Japanese].

Kumamoto Nichinichi Newspaper. (2016b, April 15). *Special edition.* Kumamoto, Japan: Kumamoto Nichinichi Newspaper [Written in Japanese].

Kumamoto Prefectural Board of Education. (2020). *The role of the chief of disaster prevention (Bosai Shunin no Yakuwari).* www.pref.kumamoto.jp/site/kyouiku/61527.html (Accessed on 16 November 2021) [Written in Japanese].

Kumamoto Prefecture. (2017). *Priority towards innovative recovery (Souzouteki Fukko ni Muketa Jutenkomoku ni Tsuite).* www.pref.kumamoto.jp/uploaded/attachment/15272.pdf (Accessed on 12 July 2021) [Written in Japanese].

Kumamoto University. (2016). *Record of Kumamoto Earthquake (Kumamoto Jishin Kirokushu), Chapter 4 towards recovery.* Kumamoto, Japan: Kumamoto University [Written in Japanese].

Mashiki Town. (2018). *Summary of Mashiki town.* www.town.mashiki.lg.jp/kiji0032000/index.html (Accessed on 14 July 2021) [Written in Japanese].

Nakanishi, H., Black, J., & Matsuo, K. (2014). Disaster resilience in transportation: Japan earthquake and tsunami 2011. *International Journal of Disaster Resilience in the Built Environment, 5*(4), 341–361. https://doi.org/10.1108/IJDRBE-12-2012-0039

Sasaki, Y., Tanaka, N., & Shibata, Y. (2020). The current situation of recovery of affected area of Kumamoto earthquake and future prospects. *Fukkou, 9*(1), 9–14 [Written in Japanese].

Suzuki, I., Suga, M., & Atsumi, T. (2003). Disasters volunteers in Japan: A historical review and the current movement since the 1995 Kobe earthquake. *The Japanese Journal of Experimental Social Psychology, 42*(2), 166–186 [Written in Japanese].

The Mainichi. (2016). *35 diagnosed with 'economy-classsyndrome' in quake-hit Kumamoto Pref. April 25, 2016 (Mainichi Japan)*. Tokyo, Japan: The Mainichi Newspapers.

6 Floods and evacuation challenges

Western Japan flood of 2018

The flood

Record-breaking precipitation occurred during the period from 28 June to 8 July 2018. The frontal depression that had stayed over north Japan since 28 June moved to the western part of Japan on the 5 July. Meanwhile, the 7th typhoon moved north over the East China Sea and was transformed into another tropical system over the Japan Sea. The frontal depression and typhoon brought 1,800mm of rain to the Shikoku area and 1,200m of rain to the east coast (Japan Meteorological Agency, 2018). The heavy rain triggered the collapse of river dykes, landslides and inundation. This flood claimed the lives of more than 220 people in the western part of Japan. More than 30,000 houses were flooded, and 11,000 houses were completely or partly destroyed. About 3,400 people moved to 168 evacuation centres (as of 7 August) rising to over 4,000 by 10 August (Cabinet Office, 2018). The most affected prefectures were Okayama, Hiroshima and Ehime[1] (Figure 6.1).

Climate change is leading to the increased possibility of frequent heavy precipitation, temperature extremes and increased maximum speed of tropical cyclones (IPCC, 2012). Japan is one of the most prepared countries for disasters, in terms of infrastructure such as dykes, warning systems (including warnings to individuals' mobile phones) and evacuation training. However, the Western Japan floods of 2018 revealed that, no matter how well infrastructure is developed, survival from hazards depends on residents' preparedness and behaviours (i.e., their decisions to evacuate and how they evacuate).

In the case of the Western Japan flood of 2018, many lives could have been saved if the risks were understood more properly and necessary actions were taken in a timely manner. The Japan Meteorological Agency and each local government issued special warnings for heavy rain and advised residents to evacuate. Experts consider that the timing

DOI: 10.4324/9781003150190-6

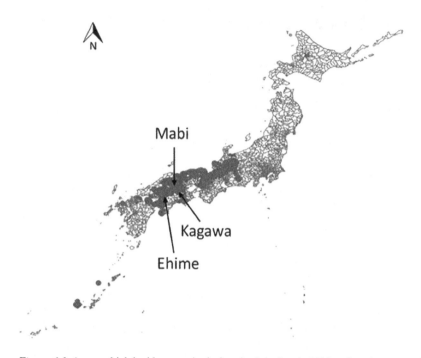

Figure 6.1 Areas which had heavy rain during the July floods 2018 and study area

Source: (Map made by the author based on 72 hours rainfall, source: Japan Meteorological Agency, 2018)

of local governments warnings and how quickly residents started evacuation were critical factors (Kakimoto & Yoshida, 2020; Nakano et al., 2019). Most victims were older people, which reveals the vulnerability of an ageing society. Many residents commented that they did not think that their houses would be flooded or they did not think that their area had had a special warning for heavy rain (Shikoku Newspaper, 8 July 2018b). In this chapter, lessons are discussed based on archival analysis and fieldwork.

Utilisation of hazard maps and warning systems

Hazard maps

Since 2005, each municipal government has been required to develop and disseminate hazard maps to residents using insights gained from the disastrous events of the previous year. Hazard maps include information on prospective hazard levels, based on scientific analysis in the hydraulic and civil engineering fields. Hazard maps are distributed to each household, are published on the websites of the municipal governments and are utilised in evacuation training. In what is regarded as a unique approach, Japanese hazard maps include 'how to act' information, based on specific depth intervals (and colours) (Van Alphen et al., 2009). The Japanese government provides an online portal where areas of risks are shown on a map, by type of hazard. The users can also layer the different types of hazards to understand the risks to their neighbourhoods.

Warning system

The Japan Meteorological Agency issues various warnings for events such as typhoons, heavy rain, earthquakes etc. Emergency warnings are intended for extraordinary phenomena. Residents who live in the area where emergency warnings are issued are recommended to take all possible steps to protect their lives.

In terms of heavy rain, the five alert levels (Table 6.1) have been provided since 2019.[2] All residents are required to evacuate when the level 4 alert is issued.

Table 6.1 Warning levels and actions to be taken

Alert level	Weather warnings/ advisories	Actions to be taken by municipalities	Actions to be taken by residents
1	Probability of warnings	Prepare for disaster Check communication method of staff	Prepare for disaster
2	Heavy rain advisory Flood advisory Storm surge advisory	Prepare for emergency response (allocate liaison staff, prepare for evacuation of the elderly)	Check evacuation action with a hazard map etc.
3	Heavy rain warning (landslide) Flood warning Storm surge advisory	Evacuation of the elderly etc. Prepare for level 4 alert	Older people, disabled people and others who may need more time to evacuate should evacuate
4	Landslide alert information Storm surge emergency warning Storm surge warning	Evacuation instruction Arrange an emergency management headquarters	All residents should evacuate before level 5 alert is issued

(Continued)

Table 6.1 (Continued)

Alert level	Weather warnings/ advisories	Actions to be taken by municipalities	Actions to be taken by residents
5	Heavy rain emergency warning	Emergency safety measures	A life-threatening situation and a safe evacuation is not possible Take any actions to save lives

(Source: author's compilation from Japan Meteorological Agency website)

The warnings are disseminated to residents through various means: a local wireless-activated disaster warning system, direct message to smartphones, TV news, radio news and the social media of local governments.

Preparation of disaster prevention plan and evacuation training

This section explores two cases to tease out the issues of preparedness and evacuation. In both cases, the affected areas match the hazard map. Why could casualties not be minimised given that the information on floods and landslides had already been distributed? The potential factors are identified through the examination of these cases.

Case of Ehime prefecture

In Ehime prefecture, the heavy rain affected the western part of the prefecture. Twenty-seven people died (plus five related deaths) and 33 people were injured. More than 130 people were rescued by fire brigades etc. In terms of loss/damages to houses, 6,619 houses were completely/partly destroyed (Ehime Prefecture, 2019). Evacuation reached its peak with 4,293 residents temporarily housed in 395 shelters across the prefecture. The dykes of the Hiji River, the main river of Ehime, collapsed and flooded the wider area of Ōzu city. In the prefecture, most lives were lost in landslides.[3] After the Meteorological Agency issued warnings of heavy rain and landslides, they used the emergency broadcast system and radio to warn residents to prepare for and start the evacuation of older people.[4] In addition, members of local fire brigades visited each house to encourage early evacuation (Ehime Prefecture, 2019). However, according to the questionnaire survey, which was conducted by the prefecture, some residents could not hear the broadcast system due to the noise of heavy rain. This caused a delay in evacuation.

In the report of the flood hazard investigation committee of the prefecture, it was discussed that 'the training of staff for flood' was not enough, because their training was more focused on the Nankai Trough earthquake at the time of the disaster (Ehime Prefecture, 2019). It was also reported that, not only at the prefecture level, but also at the national, city and town level, there was not clear instruction on when to move on to the next alert level.

The most difficult decision that residents faced was 'when' to evacuate (Ehime Prefecture, 2019). Some residents did not evacuate, even after being encouraged by the local fire brigades. It is clear from the prefecture's investigation that a significant number of residents' lives were saved because they evacuated early. However, at its peak, the proportion of residents who had evacuated was only 0.6%. Many residents evacuated the morning after peak time, after realising that their neighbourhoods were flooded. Comments from many residents such as *'staying upstairs,' 'evacuation is more dangerous'* or *'my house never flooded so it is safe'* reflect a lack of awareness of the scale of the hazard.

Case of Okayama prefecture

Mabi town, located to the city of Kurashiki, was developed alongside the Oda river, which is the tributary of the Takahashi river. Most areas of the town are surrounded by both rivers, and the town has had floods several times in the past (for example, the 1893 flood was a critical disaster, Umitsu, 2019).

In Mabi town, about 1,200 hectares were flooded over a period of three days, eight river dykes collapsed and 5,700 houses were completely or partially destroyed. In this town, 59 people lost their lives (Kurashiki City, 2019). Older people who could not evacuate were the main victims. Several dykes on the Oda river and its tributaries, such as the Suemasa and Takama rivers, broke. In addition to the backwater phenomena from the Oda river, the unique s-shape of the Suemasa river might have led to the severe flooding (Umitsu, 2019). The smaller rivers in Mabi town also experienced the backwater phenomena (Katada, 2020).

The timeline of the crisis period is as follows.[5]

On 6 July, the Emergency Management Headquarters meeting was held. The mayor requested a high level of preparedness.

11:30 An order to prepare and evacuate older people was issued in mountainous areas (preparing for landslides).

18:30 An order to prepare and evacuate older people was issued in areas around the Kurashiki river and Yoshikawa river (preparing for flood).

19:30 Advice to evacuate was issued around mountainous areas.

22:00 Advice to evacuate was issued to all areas of Mabi town.

22:40 A special warning for heavy rain was issued (for landslide).

23:10 A special warning for heavy rain was issued (for flood).

23:45 An emergent evacuation order was issued to the southern area of the Oda river (for flood).

7 July

0:00 An evacuation order was issued for the area to the west of the Takahashi river (for flood).

1:30 An emergent evacuation order was issued for the north side area of the Oda river (for flood).

1:30 An evacuation order was issued for the area alongside the Ashimori river.

4:00 An emergent evacuation order was issued for the Hiroe area (for landslide).

The evacuation order was issued at 1:30am on 7 July by the city council after the water level exceeded the dyke's height at the Takahashi River. Towards the end of the night, the dykes of another river collapsed (Shikoku Newspaper, 12 July 2018c).

There were a few questionnaire surveys conducted with residents. The results of the survey conducted by the Okayama Broadcasting Company (N=100) showed that around half of the participants did not expect that the flood would be very serious, despite the repeated warnings issued by the Meteorological Agency (Yasui et al., 2019). Only around 20% were aware of the hazard map and understood the risks. Participants who knew about hazard maps were more likely to understand the meanings of the different kinds of 'warnings,' which led them to evacuate. The result of the survey conducted by the prefecture's flood investigation committee (N=3,127) showed similar results. The result of the prefecture's survey also showed that the awareness of hazard maps was low in older people (Yasui et al., 2019).

According to the questionnaire survey conducted by Kurashiki City (Kurashiki City, 2019) targeting 2,878 households, 80% of the participants (N=1,504) responded that they heard the emergency evacuation order. However, 43% stayed at home. In terms of people over 65 years old, this proportion was 49%. Most people who evacuated to other places (i.e., shelters and other houses) started evacuation at around 22:00 (15.2%) and 23:00 (25.4%).

Most of the victims were older people (of whom 35% would have needed assistance) and were found in their houses. About 2,350 people were rescued from the rooftops or windows of their houses as a result of vertical evacuation inside of their houses. After the disaster, some grassroots activists emerged to support recovery and improve residents' awareness.

Problems with infrastructure and the built environment

In Kagawa prefecture, heavy rain was observed in the middle-west area, where river dykes were broken and landslides occurred (Japan Society of Civil Engineers West Japan Flood Investigation Taskforce, 2018). In some areas of the prefecture, total rainfall exceeded 350mm, which is unusual for one of the driest prefectures in Japan. A flood warning was issued on 6 July at 8:23 in most cities and towns in the prefecture and was only withdrawn before 5pm the next day. The warning of landslide was withdrawn on the morning of 8 July (Kagawa Prefecture, 2018). There were no deaths, but one person was injured. Ten houses were partly destroyed, and two houses were completely destroyed. At its peak time, 444 people were in evacuation shelters (Shikoku Newspaper, 8 July 2018b).[6]

Damage to infrastructure

As of 1 August 2018, 156 rivers and civil engineering infrastructure were damaged by the flood (Kagawa Prefecture, 2018, see Figure 6.2 for one of the damaged dykes of river).

Figure 6.2 Damaged dyke of river in Kagawa Prefecture
Source: (taken by the author in September 2018)

Figure 6.3 A damaged house by the landslide
Source: (taken by the author in September 2018)

The author investigated the area of Yashima where a landslide caused a collapse of ponds and one house was partly destroyed. In Kagawa prefecture, irrigation ponds (called '*Tameike*') have been developed since the Middle Ages due to the dry climate in the area. However, since the water system called *Kagawa Yosui* was developed in 1978, the irrigation ponds had been used less. In the East Yashima area, an evacuation order was issued to 136 households (299 people) (Shikoku Newspaper, 7 July 2018a). Mud flew into a house from a hill behind (Figure 6.3). Landslides also happened in the western side of Yahisma. Residents had never experienced this scale of landslide during the period they had lived there (Shikoku Newspaper, 4 August 2018f) (Figure 6.3).

The problem of tameike (irrigation ponds)

Most '*tameike*' were developed before the Edo era. They are old and need maintenance to avoid collapse. In addition, the owners of the ponds or the members of management groups are ageing or dead. When the author checked the list of the ponds in September 2018, many of their owners were already dead and no new owners were registered. At the time of the floods,

Figure 6.4 A landslide

Source: (taken by the author in September 2018)

around 50 ponds were damaged in Kagawa prefecture (Shikoku Newspaper, 5 August 2018g). The prefecture is progressing with the renovation of the ponds by identifying 289 ponds as 'prioritised ponds to be renovated to reduce hazard risks.' However, smaller ponds are not prioritised. Among these ponds, 64% were included in hazard maps and the rest were not as of July 2018 (Shikoku Newspaper, 18 July 2018e). It is important for residents to know where their nearby ponds are and discuss risks at the meeting of neighbourhood associations or local brigades.

Figure 6.5 shows a pond that had landslide. There is another pond on top of the lower one, and this two-storey pond is on top of a hill. There are houses below the ponds. If the lower-level pond collapses, the mud will flow into these houses.

The built environment (houses are built next to hills and the location of ponds) is a factor that is increasing risk. Landslides caused by this flood happened in areas where there was more granite included in the soil. Granite becomes slippery once it contains water. The soil of Kagawa prefecture contains a significant amount of granite, which enhances the risk of landslides.

Figure 6.5 Two-storey pond that had landslide
Source: (taken by the author in September 2018)

How to enhance preparedness

The 2018 flood was a warning that heavy rain is becoming more intensive and areas that have had floods in the past are being repeatedly affected. Lessons from past experience were not used effectively. No matter how much technology has advanced and how often the warning system is updated, they are ineffective unless residents take action at the right time. Human beings tend to rate risk lower than its actual level (Katada, 2020). This bias is a barrier to timely evacuation. In Mabi town, the evacuation order was issued at midnight. This is not helpful because evacuating during the night with heavy rain is even more dangerous. In particular, older people hesitate to evacuate if they do not feel confident during heavy rain or when it is dark (Nakanishi et al., 2019). If heavy rain is expected, warnings need to be issued before dark, otherwise, residents will not be able to evacuate. In addition, older people tend to wait for their family (e.g., children, if they are living in surrounding areas) to pick them up. However, their rescuers might be stranded somewhere on the way. It is too risky for them to wait until their family members arrive.

There is a limitation to how much local governments can be fully responsible for warning and protecting residents from natural hazards.

As residents used to work together in the past (Chapter 3), it is important that each resident understands that it is in fact they who can protect their own lives and decide on the appropriate behaviour. Local governments provide information about shelters and basic emergency goods and assist the most vulnerable people. However, with limited resources (in particular, in rural areas) this is the most that they can do. In an ageing society, the proportion of people who need assistance at the time of a natural hazard is increasing. Each resident, neighbourhood and network of residents needs to be fully utilised. Many Japanese people understand that they are living in a hazard-prone country. What they are lacking is the recognition that anyone can be a victim, so they need to enhance their own preparedness for disasters. The ability to enhance preparedness can be improved by gaining the skills to collect relevant information and act upon it. This is learned through risk education and drills using hypothetical situations. Communication among residents, family members, neighbourhood associations and local brigades is critical, and this can only be developed during normal times through collaborative work/events and drills. Developing 'my timeline' of behaviour would be helpful. Also, a discussion amongst family members on evacuation options would be helpful.[7]

Evacuation shelters have long been a problem. Most local governments designate school gymnasiums or community centres where evacuees lie together on floors with blankets. This lack of privacy often discourages residents from evacuating. This situation has been reviewed and some ideas have been applied since the North East Japan earthquake and tsunami of 2011. The author attended a workshop in November 2019 held in Ishinomaki, one of the affected cities by the tsunami, discussing how to make evacuation life in shelters more comfortable and reduce health risks caused by not being able to have enough space for each person to stretch out. Under the guidance of a medical doctor who is working on this matter, participants (mostly volunteers) discussed and did some experiments using cardboard partitions with beds (Figure 6.6).

After the COVID-19 pandemic, guidelines for avoiding high density situations in shelters were published by the Japan Medical Association in June 2020. It is advised that it is necessary to have at least 2m between disposable beds, to dedicate a separate route to bathrooms and to ventilate the air every 30 minutes (Japan Medical Association, 2020). This is a big challenge, as shelters have had limited space for evacuees even before the pandemic. It is recommended that the number of shelters in each jurisdiction and the capacities of each shelter be reviewed thoroughly and updated to meet the new requirements. It is emphasised that the location of shelters needs review as the scale of natural hazards becomes even more extreme. Shelters that used to be recognised as safe may no longer be viable.

Figure 6.6 Workshop discussing how to secure bedding space and partition

Source: (taken by the author in November 2019)

Notes

1 In Ehime, victims of landslides (17) were more than that of floods (8), (Ehime Prefecture, 2019)
2 The warnings system introduced in 2013 was updated in 2019. www.jma.go.jp/jma/en/Emergency_Warning/examples_of_responses.png (Japan Meteorological Agency website; written in Japanese).
3 The Seiyo city did not have a hazard map at the time of the disaster.
4 In some cities, support to older people was well prepared.
5 The warning system used was the version before the update in 2019.
6 The evacuation order was issued to 4,454 households (11,711 people) during the peak time of the afternoon of 7 July. This was the highest number in the last five years. However only 3.7 % evacuated (Shikoku Newspaper, 14 July 2018). Each local government issued the warning early so that residents could evacuate before dark.
7 Recently, the water level has risen so quickly that the call for evacuation needs to be issued earlier.

References

Cabinet Office. (2018). *Update of affected communities by the July Floods.* www.bousai.go.jp/updates/h30typhoon7/pdf/300807_h30typhoon7_01.pdf (Accessed on 16 April 2022) (Written in Japanese).

Ehime Prefecture. (2019). *Report of first responses to the flood in July 2018*. Ehime, Japan: Ehime prefecture [Written in Japanese].

IPCC. (2012). *Managing the risks of extreme events and disasters to advance climate change adaptation. A special report of working groups I and II of the intergovernmental panel on climate change* [C. B. Field, V. Barros, T. F. Stocker, D. Qin, D. J. Dokken, K. L. Ebi, M. D. Mastrandrea, K. J. Mach, G.-K. Plattner, S. K. Allen, M. Tignor, & P. M. Midgley (eds.), 582 pp]. Cambridge and New York: Cambridge University Press.

Japan Medical Association. (2020). *Emergency shelter manual (Hinanjo Manual) in the era of novel coronavirus*. Tokyo, Japan: Japan Medical Association [Written in Japanese].

Japan Meteorological Agency. (2018). *2018 July floods summary*. www.data.jma. go.jp/obd/stats/data/bosai/report/2018/20180713/20180713.html (Accessed on 16 April 2022) [Written in Japanese].

Japan Society of Civil Engineers West Japan Flood Investigation Taskforce. (2018). *Report of July 2018 flood (Shikoku area)*. Ehime, Japan: Japan Society of Civil Engineers West Japan [Written in Japanese].

Kagawa Prefecture. (2018). *Report of flood since 5 July 2018 (report no.87)*. Kagawa, Japan: Kagawa prefecture [Written in Japanese].

Kakimoto, R., & Yoshida, M. (2020). Analysis of evacuation in heavy rain based on protection motivation theory with situation awareness error. *Journal of the City Planning Institute of Japan, 55*(3), 843–850 [Written in Japanese].

Katada, T. (2020). *Hitoni yorisou bousai*. Tokyo, Japan: Shueisha Inc [Written in Japanese].

Kurashiki City. (2019). *Report of review of responses to the flood in July 2018*. Okayama, Japan: Kurashiki city [Written in Japanese].

Ministry of Land, Infrastructure, Transport and Tourism of Japan. (n.d.). *Hazard map portal site*. http://disaportal.gsi.go.jp/index.html (Accessed on 18 November 2021).

Nakanishi, H., Black, J., & Suenaga, Y. (2019). Investigating the flood evacuation behaviour of older people: A case study of a rural town in Japan. *Research in Transportation Business & Management, 30*, 100376. https://doi.org/10.1016/j. rtbm.2019.100376

Nakano, A., Nakano, S., Matsumoto, H., Nakane, D., Yamamoto, W., & Tsukai, M. (2019). Reactions of local government and of inhabitants to torrential rain disaster in Hiroshima prefecture. *Journal of Japan Society of Civil Engineers, Series B1 (Hydraulic Engineering), 75*(1), 414–428. https://doi.org/10.2208/ jscejhe.75.1_414 [Written in Japanese].

Shikoku Newspaper. (2018a). *7 July 2018 edition*. Takamatsu, Japan: Shikoku Newspaper [Written in Japanese].

Shikoku Newspaper. (2018b). *8 July 2018 edition*. Takamatsu, Japan: Shikoku Newspaper [Written in Japanese].

Shikoku Newspaper. (2018c). *12 July 2018 edition*. Takamatsu, Japan: Shikoku Newspaper [Written in Japanese].

Shikoku Newspaper. (2018d). *14 July 2018 edition*. Takamatsu, Japan: Shikoku Newspaper [Written in Japanese].

Shikoku Newspaper. (2018e). *18 July 2018 edition*. Takamatsu, Japan: Shikoku Newspaper [Written in Japanese].

Shikoku Newspaper. (2018f). *4 August 2018 edition*. Takamatsu, Japan: Shikoku News-paper [Written in Japanese].

Shikoku Newspaper. (2018g). *5 August 2018 edition*. Takamatsu, Japan: Shikoku News-paper [Written in Japanese].

Umitsu, M. (2019). Flood flows in the Mabi Town district, Kurashiki city, due to the 2018 West Japan severe flood disaster. *E-journal GEO, 14*(1), 53–59. www.jstage.jst.go.jp/article/ejgeo/14/1/14_53/_pdf/-char/ja (Accessed on 16 April 2022).

Van Alphen, J., Martini, F., Loat, R., Slomp, R., & Passchier, R. (2009). Flood risk mapping in Europe, experiences and best practices. *Journal of Flood Risk Management, 2*(4), 285–292. https://doi.org/10.1111/j.1753-318X.2009.01045.x

Yasui, T., Shinohara, A., Ota, K., & Nihei, Y. (2019). Relationship between evacuation behavior and awareness of flood hazard-map in Mabi town, Kurashiki city due to 2018 Western Japan Floods. *Journal of Japan Society of Civil Engineers, Series B1 (Hydraulic Engineering), 75*(2), 1381–1386. https://doi.org/10.2208/jscejhe.75.2_I_1381 [Written in Japanese].

7 Beyond sustainability

Society 5.0 and disaster resilience

Society 5.0 was proposed in the Fifth Science and Technology Basic Plan formulated in 2016. It was defined as '*A human-centered society that balances economic advancement with the resolution of social problems by a system that highly integrates cyberspace and physical space.*' (Government of Japan, 2021). It aims to maximise the utilisation of artificial intelligence (AI) for big data analysis (on behalf of humans) and provide feedback to humans in physical space, for a high quality of life and meeting the Sustainable Development Goals (SDGs). It has a wider scope compared with 'Industry 4.0' (Germany) and 'Industrial Internet' (USA). Disaster prevention and risk reduction is one of the core values that is expected to be further strengthened in Society 5.0.

What makes Society 5.0 different from the so-called 'information society' is that Society 5.0 needs to have an integrated system that operates throughout society, in a way that enhances quality of life from all aspects (Deguchi et al., 2020). It aims to develop a new system of mobility through innovations in physical infrastructure and data-driven cyberspace (Tada, 2018). This next generation of mobility infrastructure is based on the concept of mobility as a service (MAAS).

Society 5.0 will be a central infrastructure in addressing risks of disasters according to the government. Data related to natural hazards will be obtained from satellites, weather radar, drones, sensors in buildings, CCTV and information posted on social media etc. In Society 5.0, these data will be analysed by AI and notifications such as evacuation orders will be sent to individuals' smartphones. This will allow residents to evacuate to shelters well before the risk becomes too great. In Society 5.0, robots are expected to assist quick evacuation and drones will bring emergency goods to shelters. In addition, an open data portal would allow data sharing to be used to monitor post-disaster situations, as already implemented in San Francisco, Fukuoka and Aizuwakamatsu (Deguchi, 2020). The use of technology in

DOI: 10.4324/9781003150190-7

crisis situations is becoming more imperative in Japan due to ageing and depopulation.

However, it is true that Japan is well behind other advanced countries in terms of digital transformation. Robots and drones could be used in disaster situations, but the challenges are a) who will develop and organise the system? and b) what happens if an unexpected technological error occurs during the process of evacuation (in particular the situation where robots are assisting older people who are less flexible when facing unexpected situations)? There needs to be fundamental improvement in the current system to realise the vision of Society 5.0. It has been pointed out that the development of human resources capable of leading digital transformation is delayed in Japan (Tada, 2018). Neighbouring countries such as Taiwan demonstrated a speedy response through digital technology amid the COVID-19 pandemic (Lin et al., 2020). Japan has yet to demonstrate advanced use of technology in responding to crisis, except for improvements in weather information and forecasts.

That being said, there is an interesting project underway. The car maker Toyota launched the 'Woven City Project,' which aims to create real-world testing of a seamless, self-contained, technology-driven society with the full use of autonomous vehicles, robotics and AI. The CEO of Toyota calls the city a 'living laboratory.' The construction of Woven City started in March 2021 in Susono City, Shizuoka, which is close to Mt. Fuji. The principles behind the 'Woven City' are that it is a human-centred, living laboratory and ever-evolving. The population will start at 360 and it is expected to increase up to 2000.[1] If this experiment is successful, the seamless infrastructure network for mobility could be used for evacuation and advanced responses to natural hazards. Information from and about residents would be integrated into the infrastructure platform and those in need of help could be rescued in a timely manner. The updates of risks, available shelters and need for emergency goods will be continuously synchronised and residents will be brought to the safest available shelters, with emergency goods distributed to each shelter at the same time.

The case of Mabi town discussed in Chapter 6 showed that residents' estimation of risks was low at the time of flood, despite the repeated warnings of floods and landslides. It was also made clear that although hazard maps were distributed to all households, residents did not understand the risks properly. This issue of low risk perception could be improved by using technology. Technology can show residents what is likely to happen in their neighbourhood at the time of disaster. Virtual reality (VR), avatar and metaverse technology should be used in evacuation training. Using these technologies will make even the hypothetical situation look more realistic, and residents can get real-world experience. Some local governments, schools and companies have started to use VR for evacuation drills in Japan. If a metaverse environment is applied, more realistic training will be possible; users (residents) wear motion sensors that are synchronised to avatar activities in cyberspace and they can get a simulated experience based on their movement (Lee et al., 2021). The metaverse has much potential but is still under development in terms of application to disaster training. Advances in research and practice are expected. The equipment is currently too costly to be used at neighbourhood level – it is expected that it (including much lighter wearables such as smart glasses) will be more affordable as technology advances and as users increase. The Ministry of Land, Infrastructure, Transport and Tourism launched 'Project Plateau' in 2020. This project aims to provide an open data platform of 3D urban models. At this stage (as of February 2022), only 56 cities are identified as case study cities, but it is expected that the platform will be extended. Disaster management is one of the focuses of 'Project Plateau,' and currently four cases have been studied: a) fire evacuation in an high density metropolitan area (Tokyo), b) river flood evacuation in a rural city (Tottori), c) flood evacuation where most neighbourhoods are expected to be inundated and the only option is 'vertical evacuation' (Fukushima) and d) visualisation of disaster risks to improve hazard maps (48 cities).

As already discussed in this book, it is expected that, in the near future, Japan will have an earthquake and tsunami[2] of a scale which no one has experienced. The usual evacuation training may not be enough for residents to raise awareness and be prepared. More training/drills that represent real-world situations are imperative to reduce casualties in an ageing society. The use of advanced technology is necessary and the development of data platforms as well as human resources who can use the technology and data, and who can assist residents in using the technology, are in urgent need.[3] However, despite the development of technology, simulation products are rarely used at the community level. Advanced technology is useless if no one (or only a limited number of experts) can use it in practice. This is where Japan is weak (in particular, mid- and small-sized cities and rural areas), whilst many ideas to advance technologies have been developed over time.

The impact of COVID-19

Four years after Japan's Society 5.0 vision was announced, the COVID-19 (SARS-CoV-2) hit the world. The pandemic forced humans to change how they live and use infrastructure. In this section, the impact on Japanese society is reviewed. The first case was confirmed on 15 January 2020 in Japan in an individual who had stayed in Wuhan (Kawai, 2021). On 30 January, the Japanese Government launched the countermeasures headquarters. The timeline of main events is as follows:

2020

3 February: The cruise ship 'Diamond Princess' docked at Yokohama Port.

13 February: The first death was recorded in Kanagawa.

15 February: The first cluster was identified in Tokyo.

27 February: The Prime Minister ordered the closure of schools starting on 2 March across the country.

11 March: The World Health Organization (WHO) declared the 'pandemic.'

24 March: Postponing of the Tokyo 2020 Summer Olympics/Paralympics was announced.

1 April: A state of emergency was declared in seven prefectures (Saitama, Chiba, Tokyo, Kanagawa, Osaka, Hyogo and Fukuoka) until 6 May.

16 April: A state of emergency was issued to all areas of Japan.

22 April: The COVID-19 advisory board suggested an 80% reduction in movement by requesting citizens to stay home except for essential reasons.

24 April: 90% of schools were closed.

4 May: The state of emergency was extended until 31 May.

14 May: The state of emergency was eased in 39 prefectures.

21 May: The state of emergency was eased in three prefectures (Osaka, Kyoto and Hyogo).

25 May: The state of emergency was eased in all prefectures.

December: Vaccination started in the UK, US and Israel.

2021

February: Vaccination started for those in the medical sector.

April: Vaccination started for older people.

23 July: Tokyo 2020 Summer Olympics was held under a state of emergency.

24 August: Tokyo Paralympics was held.

Japan's case numbers seemed to be low compared with Europe and the United States. As of 21 December 2021, the United States had 50,846,828 cases and 806,459 deaths. The UK reported 11,425,657 confirmed cases and 147,679 deaths. In Japan, there were 1,729,030 confirmed cases and 18,375[4] deaths. However, the medical care system struggled to cope with the demand. For example, in Osaka, the intensive care unit (ICU) bed occupancy rate exceeded 100% at the time of the fourth wave (March–mid June, 2021) (Osaka prefecture Health and Medical Part, 2021). In terms of beds for moderate-mild symptom patients, the bed occupancy rate reached 90% during the fourth and fifth wave (June 2021).

Japan did not implement a 'lockdown' unlike many other countries. However, leaders of national and local governments asked people to 'stay home,' 'work from home' and 'not to travel to other prefectures.' Under a state of emergency, restaurants and cafes were asked to close early and not to serve alcohol, in addition to limits on the number of customers allowed to be served at the same time. The economic impact was significant. The percent change in GDP is shown in Table 7.1.

In terms of the unemployment rate, Figure 7.1 shows the trends over 2020 and 2021(until October).[5] The unemployment rate increased from February 2020 onward, and a significant increase is observed among females until July 2020. This was probably a result of the state of emergency, as many females engaged in the hospitality sector. The rate decreased between

Table 7.1 Contributions to year-over-year percent change in GDP

Jan–March 2020	April–June 2020	July–Sep 2020	Oct–Dec 2020	Jan–March 2021	April–June 2021	July–Sep 2021
−1.8%	−10.1%	−5.4%	−0.9%	−1.8%	7.3%	1.2%

(Source: Department of National Accounts Economic and Social Research Institute, Cabinet Office, Government of Japan 2021, Quarterly Estimates of GDP for July-September 2021 [Second Preliminary Estimates] FY2020 Annual Estimates of GDP)

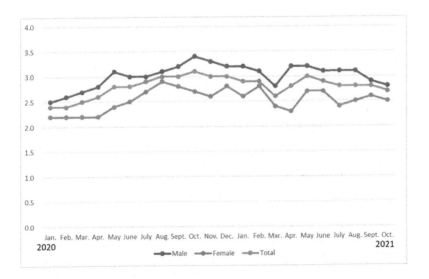

Figure 7.1 Unemployment rate

January and March of 2021, but it continued to fluctuate among females in May–June 2021. On the other hand, the male unemployment rate peaked in October 2020 and decreased gradually.

From January to December 2020, 780 bankruptcies were recorded in restaurant and café businesses, which was the highest in history (Teikoku Databank, 2021). A breakdown shows that 24.2% were restaurants/cafes/pubs/beer halls, followed by Chinese/Asian restaurants (13.5%), Western food restaurants (12.8%) and Japanese restaurants (10.1%).

In terms of the hotel/accommodation industry, nearly 90% of business owners reported in May 2020 that their bookings decreased more than 70% from the previous year (Ministry of Land, Infrastructure, Transport and Tourism, 2021). The industry recovered in November and December 2020 because of the national government's campaign 'Go to travel.' However, as the next outbreak came in January, it dropped again.

Impact on the transport sector was also enormous. In terms of air transport, booking of domestic flights dropped 93% in May 2020. It recovered later in 2020 but again dropped 75% in January 2021 (Ministry of Land, Infrastructure, Transport and Tourism, 2021). The impact on international flights was even worse. Since April 2020, bookings have reduced by 95% (Ministry of Land, Infrastructure, Transport and Tourism, 2021). Other long-distance transport such as coaches and high-speed rail were also severely affected. Public transportation as intra-transit was also seriously affected. The operation of public transportation became even more difficult in mid- and small-sized cities. As 'working from home' became more common, migration to Tokyo, which had continued over decades, stopped. In 2020, out-migration from Tokyo to surrounding areas was observed (Kinoshita, 2021). More people might be interested in living in rural areas or mid- and small-sized cities, but it is unclear if they will migrate to these areas, which would contribute to the decentralisation of population.

The economic impact was also critical for university students. The number of students who withdrew due to the pandemic was 702 in 2021 and 385 in 2020 (as of August 2021). The number of students who were on leave (as of August 2021) was 4,418 in 2021 and 2,677 in 2020 (Ministry of Education, Culture, Sports, Science and Technology, 2021).

Affected business owners and individuals received financial support under various national and local government schemes. However, various issues emerged.

The impact on the mental health of citizens was also serious. In Japan, the number of suicides had declined since 2011. However, it increased in 2020 with 21,081 cases, which was an increase of 912 from the previous year (National Police Agency, 2021). Female suicide increased significantly in 2020, notably, amongst those in their 20s. People who were not employed or not engaged in work made up nearly 50% of cases. Decisions to commit suicide are multifactored and complicated (National Police Agency, 2021). However, the pandemic, the state of emergency and the associated loss of jobs and health concerns could have led to this increase.

Towards sustainability and beyond

After achieving rapid post-war economic growth, Japan's economy became number two in the world (Chapter 3). In 1973, 90.2% of the population considered themselves middle class (Cabinet Office, 1974). However, Japan is no longer a middle-class country. It is currently facing a significant widening of the gap between the wealthy and the low socio-economic groups, after a long recession. Japan's wages have not been increasing. Japan's minimum wage (average of all prefectures) was 930 JPN an hour (8 USD) as of 2021. The prefecture with the highest minimum wage was Tokyo with 1,041 JPN an hour, and the prefectures with the lowest minimum wage of 820 JPN an hour (7.1 USD) were Kochi and Okinawa prefectures (Ministry of Health, Labor and Welfare, 2021). Japan's minimum wage level was in the middle range of Organisation for Economic Co-operation and Development (OECD) countries, in between Slovenia and Poland, in 2020.[6] Japan is still ranked third in the GDP ranking of countries, but the wage level is not at a top level. This is directly related to the poverty rate. The relative poverty rate had gradually been increasing over time and it was 15.7% in 2018. The poverty rate of children was 14.0% in 2018 (Ministry of Health, Labor and Welfare, 2019). This means one out of seven children belonged to households that were below the poverty line.

The COVID-19 pandemic seems to have contributed to the further widening of the gap between the wealthy and the low socio-economic groups. During the state of emergency, the closure of schools placed big pressures on parents. As revealed in many countries, essential workers could not work from home, and parents of those in relatively low socio-economic groups struggled to survive economically, as they lost income if they could not go to work. The business sector was asked to implement 'work from home,' but only a limited number of organisations could arrange it immediately in Japan due to the slow implementation of digitisation as mentioned previously and cultural and administrative barriers. There were still many people commuting on crowded trains, even under the state of emergency in Tokyo.

It is expected that the gap between the wealthy and non-wealthy will become even greater in the future. This divided society is extremely vulnerable in coping with natural hazards. In situations where local governments' resources will be more limited or will decrease due to ageing and the loss of a productive age population in mid- and small- sized cities, residents will be forced to rely less on governments for evacuation and relief. The most vulnerable people in this circumstance are those in low socio-economics groups, which include not only older people but also single-parent households (see Chapter 3). The aforementioned advanced technology can be more effective when local governments, no matter how financially stable or not, can access these convenient tools. There is a need for support from the national government for mid- and small-sized cities in enhancing disaster preparedness in this divided society.

Sustainability is only achieved when the quality of life of residents is secured. The author developed quality of life indicators to assess infrastructure planning. It was identified that better quality of life relies on 'safety and security,'[7] which is a basic need for life (Doi et al., 2006). As shown in Chapter 2, Japan has had natural hazards of various scales regularly. Economic growth was compensating for loss caused by natural hazards until the recession in the 1990s started. However, most responses were improvements and the development of hard infrastructure such as dykes and drainage systems, which require updates regularly. This model of investing in hard infrastructure worked when Japan was experiencing growth both in population and the economy. However, many local governments of mid- and small-sized cities are currently struggling to meet the cost of these hard infrastructure updates as natural hazards' impacts are getting more severe due to the changing climate. In this context, investing in hard infrastructure is no longer feasible. In addition, recent hazards demonstrate that this infrastructure cannot always protect residents' lives and neighbourhoods. As mentioned earlier and in previous chapters, enhancing the awareness and preparedness of residents is the most necessary approach rather than building more infrastructure.

After the North East Japan earthquake and tsunami, the national government's Central Disaster Management Council published a 'Report of the Committee for Technical Investigation on Countermeasures for Earthquakes and Tsunamis, Based on the Lessons Learned from the 2011 Earthquake off the Pacific coast of Tohoku' (Cabinet Office, 2011). In the report, tsunamis were categorised as levels 1 and 2. Level 1 tsunamis are defined to 'occur once in several decades or every hundred years.' The more catastrophic, but far less frequent tsunami is classified as 'Level 2' and is defined as 'well above the size of a Level 1 tsunami and beyond the capacity of physical infrastructure'. The tsunami triggered by the 2011 Great East Japan Earthquake is considered to belong to Level 2. It is predicted that Level 1 tsunamis will occur in the next 30 years with a 90% of possibility in the affected area. Some local governments have decided to prepare for a 'Level 1' disaster, which involves seawall (dyke) development, land use change (land readjustment and levelling) and transport network improvements (for

Figure 7.2 Seawall under construction
Source: (taken by the author in July 2019)

evacuation and emergency supplies logistics) and relocation of residents to higher grounds. Many residents, particularly in fishing villages, showed strong opposition to the seawall plan. However, many villages ended up accepting the plan, fearing that if they continued discussion, the recovery of the whole area would be delayed. Some villages negotiated the height of the seawalls, but they are still of a significant size.

The author visited Ogatsu town, Miyagi prefecture, with a group of local residents in July 2019. A seawall of nearly 10m was under construction (Figures 7.2 and 7.3). Although the construction was not completed, the scale of it was already enormous.

The sea can only be seen from the hill, and if the wall is completed, only part of the bay will be visible. The concrete structure requires regular maintenance. This is not a sustainable approach. Although the initial cost of seawall development was paid for by the national government, the maintenance cost will be paid by local communities. This is an expensive infrastructure to maintain for the next generation, as the lifespan of concrete is around 50 years, and the area is facing depopulation. There is a question mark

Figure 7.3 View of the seawall from higher ground
Source: (taken by the author in July 2019)

around whether selecting the seawall option would enhance preparedness in the future. The seawall cannot protect communities. A tsunami of more than 20m was recorded in some areas. If this happens again, the water will come over the wall and the residents, who cannot see the sea due to the wall, may be late to evacuate and be caught by the waves. The age of relying on physical (concrete) infrastructure is over. The author is not claiming that there is no need for local governments to invest in disaster risk reduction. What is necessary for the future is to invest in social infrastructure such as social capital and networks between residents to enhance preparedness together. Local governments' roles are to establish a framework where residents can build networks and to support these connections rather than maintaining physical infrastructure. This role will be more critical as ageing accelerates in the near future. The 'trust' that residents had with neighbours in agriculture-based communities before modernisation no longer exists. Reciprocity and associated behaviours to help each other at the time of natural hazards do not emerge where there is no trust between residents. A sustainable future will depend on how communities can evolve without losing their sense of belonging, sense of place and relationships and networks with neighbours.

Notes

1 According to Woven City's website: www.woven-city.global/.
2 Nankai Trough earthquakes occur every 100 to 150 years. The area affected is between Suruga Warf (Shizuoka) and Hyuganada (Miyazaki), where the Eurasian and Philippine Sea plates connect. As the last quake was in 1944, another is expected to occur in the near future, and tsunamis of more than 20m are expected to hit Japanese cities along the Pacific Ocean.
3 Start-up companies such as 'One Concern' (https://oneconcern.com/en/) are emerging. A Japanese city is using their service and there are many other services available.
4 According to the Johns Hopkins University Coronavirus Resource Center (https://coronavirus.jhu.edu/).
5 Sourced from the portal site of the Statistics Bureau of Japan. www.e-stat.go.jp/ (written in Japanese).
6 Data extracted from OECD Stat. Real minimum wages. https://stats.oecd.org/Index.aspx?DataSetCode=RMW Accessed on 16 April 2022.
7 Refers to a high level of preparedness for natural hazards and a community free from crimes.

References

Cabinet Office. (1974). *Public opinion survey concerning people's lifestyles*. Tokyo, Japan: Government of Japan [Written in Japanese].

Cabinet Office. (2011). *Report of the committee for technical investigation on countermeasures for earthquakes and tsunamis based on the lessons learned from the 2011 off the Pacific coast of Tohoku Earthquake*. Tokyo, Japan: Government of Japan [Written in Japanese].

Deguchi, A. (2020). From smart city to society 5.0. In *Society 5.0: A people-centric super-smart society* (pp. 43–65). Tokyo, Japan: Hitachi-UTokyo Laboratory.

Deguchi, A., Hirai, C., Matsuoka, H., Nakano, T., Oshima, K., Tai, M., & Tani, S. (2020). What is society 5.0. In *Society 5.0: A people-centric super-smart society* (pp. 1–23). Tokyo, Japan: Hitachi-U Tokyo Laboratory.

Department of National Accounts Economic and Social Research Institute, Cabinet Office, Government of Japan. (2021). *Quarterly estimates of GDP for July-September 2021(second preliminary estimates) FY2020 annual estimates of GDP*. Tokyo, Japan: Government of Japan [Written in Japanese].

Doi, K., Nakanishi, H., Sugiyama, I., & Shibata, H. (2006). Development of a QoL-based multi-dimensional evaluation system for urban infrastructure planning. *Japan Society of Civil Engineers: Journal of Infrastructure Planning and Management D, 62*(3), 288–303. https://doi.org/10.2208/jscejd.62.288 [Written in Japanese].

Government of Japan. (2021, March 26). *Science, technology, and innovation basic plan*. Tokyo, Japan: Government of Japan.

Kawai, K. (2021). *Document: Covid-19 advisory board meetings (Bunsuirei Document Corona Taisaku Senmonka Kaigi)*. Tokyo, Japan: Iwanami Shoten Publishers (the translation of the title is made by the author) [Written in Japanese].

Kinoshita, S. (2021). Regional economy and migration under pandemic. *JA Kyosai Research Institute, 83*(9), 6–17 [Written in Japanese].

Lee, S., Ha, G., Kim, H., & Kim, S. (2021). A collaborative serious game for fire disaster evacuation drill in metaverse. *Journal of Platform Technology, 9*(3), 70–77.

Lin, C., Braund, W. E., Auerbach, J., Chou, J. H., Teng, J. H., Tu, P., & Mullen, J. (2020). Policy decisions and use of information technology to fight COVID-19. *Emerging Infectious Diseases, 26*(7), 1506–1512. https://doi.org/10.3201/eid2607.200574

Ministry of Education, Culture, Sports, Science and Technology. (2021). *Urgent subsidy to support students. Related materials 20 December 2021.* www.mext.go.jp/content/20211222-mxt_gakushi01-000019288_8.pdf (Accessed on 28 December 2021) [Written in Japanese].

Ministry of Health, Labor and Welfare. (2019). *Result of comprehensive survey of living conditions. December, 2021.* Tokyo, Japan: Ministry of Health, Labor and Welfare [Written in Japanese].

Ministry of Health, Labor and Welfare. (2021). *Minimum wage updates of each prefecture.* Tokyo, Japan: Ministry of Health, Labor and Welfare [Written in Japanese].

Ministry of Land, Infrastructure, Transport and Tourism. (2021). *White paper 2021.* Tokyo, Japan: Ministry of Land, Infrastructure, Transport and Tourism [Written in Japanese].

National Police Agency. (2021). *Situation of suicides in 2020. Published on 16 March 2021.* www.npa.go.jp/safetylife/seianki/jisatsu/R03/R02_jisatuno_joukyou.pdf (Accessed on 16 April 2022) [Written in Japanese].

Osaka Prefecture Health and Medical Part. (2021, October 21). *Report of infection and responses from the first wave to fifth wave.* Osaka, Japan: Osaka Prefectural Government [Written in Japanese].

Tada, W. (2018). *AI underdeveloped country: The key is to develop human resources in deep learning sector (AI Koshin Koku).* Tokyo, Japan: Nikkei BP (the translation of the title is made by the author) [Written in Japanese].

Teikoku Databank. (2021). *Survey result of bankrupt trend of restaurant/cafes 2020.* Tokyo, Japan: Teikoku Databank, Ltd. [Written in Japanese].

8 Conclusion

Through interviews and conversations with residents, this book showed that residents are very concerned about their financial stability in the future due to societal change and the increasing poverty rate. In Chapter 3, the comments of young adults were discussed and financial security was revealed to be their main concern. My perception of Japanese people is consistent with the result of the World Happiness Report (Helliwell et al., 2020). The report shows that Japan is ranked 62nd in the Ranking of Happiness 2017–2019. This ranking is based on the subjective well-being of citizens and how the social, urban and natural environments combine to affect their happiness. The top five countries were Finland, Denmark, Switzerland, Iceland and Norway. More European and Oceania countries follow. This is just one indicator, but this clearly shows that Japanese citizens are not happy compared with other developed countries, and their concern for the future is affecting the result. The economy has yet to recover after the COVID-19 pandemic hit. The depreciation of the Japanese yen in global markets and associated rise of commodity prices (as of April 2022), plus the Ukraine crisis that started in late February, are all negatively impacting happiness.

Clearly, Japan's challenges are the state of the economy, the ageing of the population, the low birth rate and the imbalanced concentration of population and business in metropolitan areas. All this is accompanied by series of naturally occurring crises. To meet the challenges, citizens need to have a better quality of life. Recently, in the urban development field (both theory and practice), the concept of 'smart cities'[1] is often discussed and many cities are attempting transformations through schemes such as 'Smart City Strategy' or 'Smart Model Cities.' However, 'Smart Cities' or technology-driven cities are not a universal solution. The author agrees with Green (2019) who states that 'the view through tech goggles, that it is possible to create optimal cities using new technology, diverts attention away from and subverts opportunities to democratically and equitably improve cities' (p. 185). In this context, even 'Society 5.0' is not a solution. Both 'Smart Cities' and 'Society 5.0'

DOI: 10.4324/9781003150190-8

are too driven by idealism and lack a human-scale approach that addresses Japan's societal issues. The important indicator of urban development is how improvements in living environments contribute to a better quality of life for its users, that is, citizens/residents. Digital technology is one of the tools that contributes to the improvement of living environments, but it does not solve all the issues. Urban development needs to contribute to a better quality of life through harmonised improvement of infrastructure and society.

As I wrote in Chapter 7, 'safety and security' is a basic need to achieve a better quality of life. However, this element alone does not satisfy our happiness. Social connections and social capital are also important, as discussed in Chapters 3 and 7. In this context, the core value of urban development should be a) disaster resilience as an essential element of society and b) quality of life. Social capital strongly influences disaster resilience (Figure 8.1). Economically deprived societies often lack social capital because lack of financial security takes away opportunities to participate in community activities. A 'sense of belonging to a neighbourhood' and residents' feelings that 'they can trust people' are strongly related to social capital and community involvement (Doi et al., 2006). The agriculture-based community in pre-modern Japan did not need financial security to have social capital. The agriculture/farming lifestyle naturally allowed residents to collaborate and trust each other. However, in the contemporary lifestyle where most people engage in paid work outside of their neighbourhood, there are limited opportunities for them to meet and participate in common activities. Neighbourhood associations and school-based activities used to provide such opportunities, but in many places in Japan, many people no longer belong to these groups and residents do not know their neighbours (even their next-door neighbours).

Technology is helpful in assisting people in responding to natural hazards, and for practitioners, it is an important tool for data collection. However, to make the most use of technology, society needs to already be resilient, and this can only be achieved by social capital and financial security. Financial security is not about making profits by development; it is more about residents having comfortable lives without serious economic concerns and an adequate support system if necessary. Currently, Japanese cities are undergoing a wave of development of high-rise apartment buildings, although the total population is decreasing. Urban development that seeks only short-term profit without a clear long-term vision will not nurture social capital. As Jacobs (1961) wrote, competition based on retail profitability is most apt to affect streets or even whole districts. 'A most intricate and successful organism of economic mutual support and social mutual support has been destroyed by the process' (Jacobs, 1961, p. 243). This is exactly what has happened in Japan recently.

We now have enough evidence that current urban development is not producing resilient cities. It is time to stop and reconsider what is most

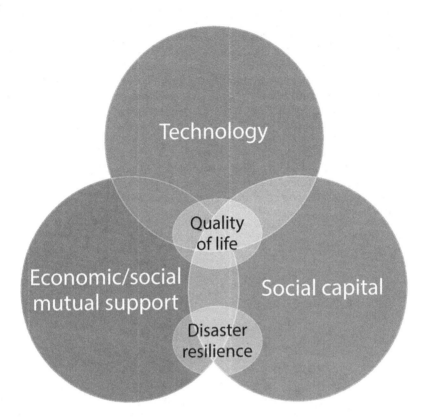

Figure 8.1 Core value of urban development

important for our society. 'Cities are an immense laboratory of trial and error, failure and success in city building and city design' (Jacob, 1961, p. 6). In the age of crisis, both urban planners and residents need to trial new and different approaches. Collaborative urban development which focuses on quality of life will enhance disaster resilience.

Note

1 According to Batty (2012), 'The idea of integrating much of this diverse data* together to add value to our conceptions of how it might be linked to other more traditional data as well as focusing it on specific ways to make cities more efficient and more equitable, has come to define the 'smart cities movement.' *Data refers to information about many different kinds of objects for the purposes of entertainment, advertising and serious pursuits involving work-day activities.

References

Batty, M. (2012). Smart cities, big data. *Environment and Planning B: Planning and Design, 39*(2), 191–193. https://doi.org/10.1068/b3902ed

Doi, K., Nakanishi, H., Morishita, K., & Sugiyama, I. (2006). Quality of life, social capital and community asset management. In K. Ito, H. Westlund, K. Kobayashi, & T. Hatori (Eds.), *Social capital and development trends in rural areas* (Vol. 2, 205–225). Kyoto, Japan: MARG, Kyoto University Press.

Green, B. (2019). *The smart enough city: Putting technology in its place to reclaim our urban future*. Cambridge, MI: MIT Press.

Helliwell, J. F., Layard, R., Sachs, J., & De Neve, J. E. (2020). *World happiness report 2020*. New York: Sustainable Development Solutions Network. https://worldhappiness.report/ed/2020/ (Accessed on 16 April 2022).

Jacobs, J. (1961). *The death and life of great American cities*. New York: Random House, Inc.

Index

Note: Page numbers in italics indicate figures and page numbers in bold indicate tables.

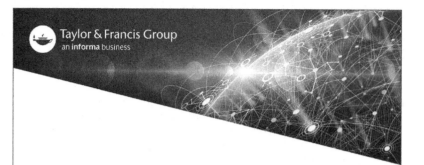